CRICKET & CORPORATE: Management Lessons From The Pitch

Dr. Munir A Chandniwala

Qurate
quratebooks.com

CRICKET & CORPORATE MANAGEMENT LESSONS FROM THE PITCH

Dr. Munir A. Chandniwala

Published in 2025

© Published by

Qurate
qurate books.com

Qurate Books Pvt. Ltd.
Goa 403523, India
www.quratebooks.com
Tel: 1800-210-6527, Email: info@quratebooks.com

ISBN: 978-93-58988-26-0

PREFACE

Cricket is more than just a sport—it is a way of life that embodies strategy, teamwork, adaptability, and leadership. From the bustling streets of gully cricket to the grand stadiums where international players showcase their talent, every game holds lessons far beyond the boundary line. Interestingly, many of these lessons are directly applicable to the world of corporate management.

In my years of observing and analyzing both cricket and corporate dynamics, I have realized that the fundamental principles that make a cricket team successful—leadership, coordination, delegation, communication, execution, and time management—are the same principles that drive successful organizations. Just as a cricket captain must make split-second decisions under pressure, a corporate leader must navigate uncertainties and guide their team toward victory. A well-balanced playing XI is akin to a high-performing corporate team where each member has a specific role, and success depends on synergy rather than individual brilliance alone.

Many of us have played and watched cricket. Is easy to connect with cricket and corporate world what we have been doing since we were young. This book is an attempt to bridge the gap between the cricket field and the corporate boardroom, drawing parallels between strategies used by legendary cricketers and those required for effective management. Whether it's handling crises like a middle-order collapse or managing resources in a long-format Test match, the wisdom from cricket can offer invaluable insights for professionals across industries.

Through real-life match scenarios, historic cricketing moments, and practical corporate applications, this book will serve as a guide for managers, executives, and corporate employees striving to improve their leadership skills, teamwork, and strategic thinking. Whether you are a seasoned professional, an aspiring manager, or simply a cricket enthusiast, I hope these lessons help you gain a fresh perspective on management through the lens of the game we all love.

Let's step onto the pitch and play this corporate innings with the spirit of cricket!

Dr. Munir A. Chandniwala
(B.pharm, MBA, Mphil, PhD)

CONTENTS

Chapter 1

INTRODUCTION: THE CRICKET-MANAGEMENT PARALLEL

How Cricket Mirrors the Corporate World: A Management Perspective

Cricket is more than just a sport; it is a game of strategy, teamwork, leadership, and decision-making. Interestingly, the corporate world operates on similar principles. The dynamics of cricket mirror the realities of the business environment, where planning, execution, adaptability, and resilience are crucial. This article explores how cricket reflects the corporate world through various managerial aspects, with real-world examples from both domains.

1. Leadership and Captaincy: The Role of CEOs

A cricket team's captain is akin to a company's CEO. The captain sets the vision, motivates players, and makes crucial on-field decisions, just as a CEO steers the company's direction, inspires employees, and makes strategic business decisions.

Example:

- **Cricket:** MS Dhoni's calm demeanor and ability to make crucial decisions under pressure led India to multiple victories, including the 2007 T20 World Cup and the 2011 ODI World Cup.
- **Corporate:** Satya Nadella transformed Microsoft by adopting a growth mindset, encouraging innovation, and leading the company into the cloud computing era.

2. Teamwork and Collaboration: Departmental Synergy

Cricket is a team sport where every player contributes to the overall success, just like an organization where different departments work together to achieve business objectives.

Example:

- **Cricket:** The 2019 ICC Cricket World Cup final saw England's entire team contribute—Ben Stokes with his batting, Jofra Archer's super over, and Jos Buttler's match-winning run-out.
- **Corporate:** Apple's success in launching the iPhone depended on synergy between hardware designers,

software engineers, marketing experts, and supply chain managers.

3. Strategy and Planning: Business Roadmap

Cricket matches require meticulous planning based on the opposition's strengths and weaknesses. Similarly, businesses must analyze competitors and market trends before making strategic decisions.

Example:

- **Cricket:** Before the 2001 Kolkata Test, India devised a strategy to counter Australia's aggressive play, leading to a historic comeback win.
- **Corporate:** Netflix shifted from DVD rentals to streaming services, adapting its strategy to evolving consumer preferences and technological advancements.

4. Adaptability: Playing in Different Conditions

Cricketers must adapt to different playing conditions—pitch, weather, and opposition strategies. Likewise, businesses must adjust to economic conditions, customer demands, and technological changes.

Example:

- **Cricket:** Virat Kohli adjusted his batting technique when playing in England, where swing bowling is a major challenge.
- **Corporate:** Nokia, which failed to adapt to the smartphone era, lost its market dominance, whereas companies like Samsung and Apple innovated and thrived.

5. Risk Management: Calculated Risks in Decision-Making

A cricket team often takes calculated risks, such as sending a pinch-hitter up the order or deploying an attacking field. Businesses, too, take risks when entering new markets or launching new products.

Example:

- **Cricket:** In the 2007 T20 World Cup final, MS Dhoni gambled by giving the last over to Joginder Sharma, which ultimately won India the title.
- **Corporate:** Tesla's early investment in electric vehicles was a massive risk, but it paid off, positioning the company as a market leader in EV technology.

6. Performance Under Pressure: Crisis Management

Pressure situations in cricket test players' mental strength, just as businesses face crises that demand quick and effective decision-making.

Example:

- **Cricket:** Ben Stokes' remarkable innings in the 2019 Ashes Test at Headingley, where he single-handedly led England to victory under immense pressure.
- **Corporate:** PepsiCo's response to the pesticide controversy in India by launching a transparent PR campaign to regain consumer trust.

7. Continuous Improvement: Training and Up skilling

Cricketers undergo rigorous training, learn new skills, and analyze past performances to improve. Similarly, companies invest in employee training and development to stay competitive.

Example:

- **Cricket:** Sachin Tendulkar continuously refined his technique to remain at the top for over two decades.
- **Corporate:** Google provides continuous learning opportunities for its employees to encourage innovation and skill enhancement.

8. Talent Identification and Grooming: Succession Planning

Cricket teams scout young talent and groom them for future roles. Businesses also identify and nurture high-potential employees for leadership positions.

Example:

- **Cricket:** The Australian Cricket Academy has produced legends like Ricky Ponting and Michael Clarke.
- **Corporate:** Companies like IBM and Unilever have robust leadership development programs that groom future CEOs.

9. Data-Driven Decisions: Use of Analytics

Modern cricket relies on data analytics for player performance, pitch conditions, and opponent strategies. Similarly, businesses use big data and analytics for decision-making.

Example:

- **Cricket:** Teams use analytics to determine optimal field placements and bowling strategies based on an opponent's weaknesses.
- **Corporate:** Amazon uses AI-driven recommendations to enhance customer experience and drive sales.

10. Brand and Reputation Management

A cricket team's reputation depends on its performance and conduct. Similarly, businesses must uphold their brand image and maintain stakeholder trust.

Example:

- **Cricket:** The ball-tampering scandal tarnished Australia's image, leading to leadership changes and a cultural shift in the team.
- **Corporate:** Volkswagen's emissions scandal led to a major reputational crisis, requiring the company to implement corrective measures.

Cricket and the corporate world share numerous similarities in leadership, strategy, teamwork, adaptability, risk management, and performance under pressure. The lessons learned from cricket can be effectively applied in business environments to build strong organizations, make strategic decisions, and drive success. Whether on the field or in the boardroom, the principles of planning, execution, resilience, and continuous improvement remain fundamental to achieving excellence.

From Gully Cricket to Professional Leagues - Evolution of Skills & Leadership

Management Lesson: Growth, adaptability, and leadership emerge through experience and challenges.

Cricket Example: The journey of players like Virat Kohli, Bumrah, Waqar Younus who transitioned from street cricket to international stardom.

Gully cricket, often played in narrow lanes with limited resources, is the foundation for many aspiring cricketers. It teaches adaptability—using a makeshift bat, playing on uneven pitches, and adjusting to unpredictable conditions. This is similar to the early stages of an entrepreneur or a manager, where resource constraints demand creativity and quick decision-making.

As players move to structured club cricket, they learn discipline, teamwork, and leadership. Captaining a local team brings early experiences in strategy and man-management, much like a young professional stepping into leadership roles. The transition to state-level and professional leagues requires greater commitment, rigorous training, and the ability to perform under pressure—key attributes for corporate leadership.

The journey from gully cricket to professional leagues mirrors an individual's corporate growth, where raw talent must be honed with skills, mentorship, and experience. Leadership traits develop over time as responsibilities increase, decisions become more impactful, and teamwork becomes crucial for success.

The Importance of Teamwork, Strategy, and Adaptability

Management Lesson: Success in any organization or team depends on synergy, planning, and the ability to adjust to changing situations.

Cricket Example: The 2019 World Cup final between England and New Zealand.

Teamwork: The Foundation of Success

Cricket is not an individual sport; it thrives on the collective effort of all 11 players, much like an organization depends on its workforce. A team with talented individuals will fail if players do not collaborate and support each other. Similarly, in business, a company's success hinges on different departments working cohesively.

Example:

In the 2019 World Cup final, England demonstrated remarkable teamwork. Ben Stokes' crucial partnerships with Jos Buttler and the lower order showcased how individual brilliance alone is not enough; support from teammates is essential to victory. This aligns with corporate teamwork, where collaboration between departments leads to success in projects and business goals.

Key corporate takeaways:

- Clearly defined roles enhance team efficiency.
- Mutual trust between team members improves performance.
- A positive team culture fosters resilience and innovation.

Strategy: The Blueprint for Winning

Cricket teams do not win by chance—they analyze opponents, study pitch conditions, and devise strategies. Similarly, businesses must research competitors, assess market conditions, and plan their moves meticulously.

Example:

The way MS Dhoni planned the 2011 World Cup final, promoting himself up the order to counter Sri Lanka's spinners, was a masterstroke. He assessed the situation, identified the challenge, and executed a well-thought-out strategy, leading to a historic win. Similarly, successful companies like Apple or Amazon thrive because of their strategic planning and foresight.

- Key corporate takeaways:
- Data-driven decision-making leads to better outcomes.

- Adapting strategies based on competitors and market changes is crucial.
- Leaders must anticipate challenges and plan accordingly.

Adaptability: Thriving in a Changing Environment

Conditions in cricket can change within minutes—pitch conditions, weather, and match situations demand flexibility. Similarly, corporate environments are dynamic, requiring companies and leaders to pivot strategies when necessary.

Example:

The rise of T20 cricket revolutionized the sport. Traditional Test cricketers had to adapt their game to stay relevant. Virat Kohli, for instance, transformed his approach to succeed in all formats, balancing aggression with technique. Similarly, businesses that fail to adapt—like Nokia or Kodak—struggle, while those that evolve—like Netflix—thrive.

- Key corporate takeaways:
- Being open to change keeps businesses relevant.
- Employees and leaders must develop a growth mindset.
- Learning new skills and embracing innovation drive success.

Chapter 2

LEADERSHIP: THE CAPTAIN'S MINDSET

Management Lesson: Leadership is about decision-making, vision, and motivation.

Cricket Example: MS Dhoni's calm and composed captaincy in the 2011 World Cup final.

Great leaders, whether in cricket or corporate management, do not just instruct—they inspire. A successful captain is much like a corporate CEO, setting the direction, taking responsibility, and making tough decisions under pressure. Leadership in both fields demands vision, strategic thinking, adaptability, and the ability to bring out the best in the team.

1. Leading from the Front

One of the most crucial traits of leadership is leading by example. Whether it is the cricket field or the corporate world, people look up to their leader's performance and attitude.

Example:

- **MS Dhoni in the 2011 World Cup Final:** When India was under pressure in the final against Sri Lanka, Dhoni promoted himself up the batting order, taking responsibility and playing a match-winning knock. His calm demeanor under pressure and ability to take charge in critical moments is a hallmark of great leadership.
- **Corporate Parallel:** In times of crisis, CEOs like Steve Jobs and Satya Nadella have shown how leading from the front can inspire teams. Jobs took charge of Apple's turnaround in the late 90s by personally involving himself in product development and strategic direction, much like a captain guiding his team through tough situations.

2. Strategic Decision-Making Under Pressure

A great captain, much like a corporate leader, must make quick, calculated decisions under immense pressure.

Example:

- **Eoin Morgan's leadership in the 2019 Cricket World Cup:** Under Morgan's captaincy, England transformed their approach to white-ball cricket. By fostering an aggressive yet balanced strategy, he led his team to their first-ever World Cup victory, demonstrating the importance of strategic adaptability.

- **Corporate Parallel:** Business leaders must make crucial decisions with limited time and information. Jeff Bezos' strategic decision to transition Amazon from an online bookstore to a full-fledged e-commerce giant is a perfect example of forward-thinking leadership.

3. Empowering the Team & Delegation

Great captains trust their team members and delegate responsibilities based on individual strengths.

Example:

- **Rohit Sharma's captaincy in IPL:** Rohit has led Mumbai Indians to multiple IPL titles by trusting his bowlers to deliver in pressure situations. He gives players the freedom to express themselves while ensuring the team follows a common goal.
- **Corporate Parallel:** In management, leaders must trust their team and delegate responsibilities wisely. A successful CEO does not micromanage but empowers department heads and managers to execute strategies effectively.

4. Adaptability – Changing Strategies on the Go

Leadership is about adjusting strategies based on situations, whether in cricket or business.

Example:

- **Virat Kohli's adaptability in different formats:** Kohli has mastered Test, ODI, and T20 cricket, adjusting his game play based on the demands of each format. His ability to switch strategies is a testament to leadership versatility.
- **Corporate Parallel:** Netflix, initially a DVD rental company, pivoted to streaming and later to content creation. Like a cricket captain adjusting to pitch conditions, business leaders must recognize market trends and adapt accordingly.

5. Handling Failures and Bouncing Back

A true leader is defined not by success alone but by how they handle failures.

Example:

- **Ben Stokes' Redemption:** After his heartbreak in the 2016 T20 World Cup final, Stokes worked on his game and returned stronger, playing a crucial role in England's 2019 World Cup win.
- **Corporate Parallel:** Elon Musk faced multiple failures before Tesla and Space X became industry leaders. His resilience mirrors that of an athlete who learns from past mistakes and returns stronger.

Key Takeaways for Corporate Leaders:

- **Lead by Example:** Inspire teams with actions, not just words.
- **Strategic Decision-Making:** Assess risks and make calculated choices.
- **Empower Your Team:** Trust and delegate for efficiency.
- **Be Adaptable:** Change strategies based on circumstances.
- **Learn from Failures:** Treat setbacks as stepping stones to success.

From Cricket Captains to Corporate CEOs

Cricket captains and corporate leaders share the same fundamental responsibilities—leading teams, making tough decisions, adapting to challenges, and inspiring those around them. Whether it's Dhoni's calmness under pressure, Kohli's aggressive leadership, or Morgan's strategic planning, the lessons from cricket leadership are directly applicable to corporate management.

By embracing these principles, business leaders can build winning teams, foster innovation, and drive organizations toward success—just like a great cricket captain does on the field.

How Great Cricket Captains Lead by Example

Management Lesson: True leaders inspire their teams by setting personal examples, making sacrifices, and demonstrating resilience in the face of challenges.

A great captain does not merely dictate instructions; they embody the values and ethics that they wish their team to adopt. Leadership in cricket is much like corporate leadership—it requires leading from the front, inspiring confidence, and setting high standards through personal performance. Captains who lead by example gain the respect of their teammates, creating an environment of trust and unity.

1. Leading with Performance

Example: Virat Kohli's Work Ethic and Fitness Revolution

Virat Kohli transformed Indian cricket by setting a new benchmark for fitness and professionalism. His discipline, both on and off the field, encouraged an entire generation of players to prioritize fitness, ultimately improving the team's performance. His relentless pursuit of excellence mirrors the way corporate leaders inspire employees by demonstrating hard work and setting high standards.

Corporate Parallel: Leaders like Elon Musk and Tim Cook are known for their incredible work ethic, often putting in long hours and immersing themselves in product development. This hands-on approach inspires employees to push their own limits and strive for higher achievements.

2. Staying Calm Under Pressure

Example: MS Dhoni's Composure in Critical Moments

One of the hallmarks of Dhoni's captaincy was his ability to remain calm in high-pressure situations. Whether it was the 2011 World Cup final or a tense IPL match, Dhoni never let emotions dictate his decisions. This ability to stay composed and make rational choices under pressure is crucial in both cricket and corporate leadership.

Corporate Parallel: A CEO facing financial downturns or high-stakes negotiations must remain composed and make data-driven decisions. Leaders like Warren Buffett, known for their steady approach during market crashes, exemplify the importance of keeping emotions in check.

3. Making Personal Sacrifices for the Team

Example: Ricky Ponting's Selflessness in the 2003 World Cup Final

Despite being one of the most aggressive players of his time, Ponting often made tactical sacrifices for the benefit of the team. His captain's innings in the 2003 World Cup final, where he scored an unbeaten 140, demonstrated his willingness to take responsibility when it mattered most.

Corporate Parallel: In the business world, leaders often need to make personal sacrifices for long-term success. Indra Nooyi, former CEO of PepsiCo, made significant changes in the company's product lineup, facing criticism but ensuring long-term sustainability.

4. Building Team Morale and Trust

Example: Eoin Morgan's Leadership in the 2019 World Cup'

Morgan played a crucial role in fostering a culture of trust and empowerment, allowing players like Ben Stokes and Jos Buttler to express themselves freely. This led to England's first-ever World Cup victory.

Corporate Parallel: Corporate leaders must cultivate an environment where employees feel valued and empowered. Leaders like Richard Branson focus on employee well-being, leading to high morale and improved performance.

5. Standing by Their Team in Tough Times

Example: Sourav Ganguly's Support for Young Talent

When Sourav Ganguly took over as India's captain, he backed young players like Yuvraj Singh, Harbhajan Singh, and Virender Sehwag, giving them confidence and opportunities to shine.

Corporate Parallel: In the business world, leaders who invest in employee development and mentorship create stronger, more loyal teams. Satya Nadella's leadership at Microsoft, where he emphasized employee growth and cultural change, has led to significant success.

Key Takeaways for Corporate Leaders:

- **Set the Example:** Employees look up to leaders who practice what they preach.
- **Stay Composed Under Pressure:** Rational decisions drive long-term success.
- **Make Sacrifices for the Team:** The best leaders prioritize collective success over personal gain.
- **Build a Supportive Culture:** Employees thrive in an environment of trust and encouragement.
- **Develop Future Leaders:** Investing in the next generation ensures sustained success.

Making Tough Calls Under Pressure

Management Lesson: Effective leaders make high-stakes decisions with confidence, even under extreme pressure.

In both cricket and business, leaders are often faced with situations that require split-second decision-making. The ability to assess risks, trust one's judgment, and take bold decisions under pressure is what separates good leaders from great ones.

1. Trusting Your Instincts in Critical Moments

Cricket Example: MS Dhoni's Decision to Bowl Joginder Sharma in the 2007 T20 World Cup Final

During the final over of the 2007 T20 World Cup, MS Dhoni made a bold decision by handing the ball to an inexperienced Joginder Sharma instead of the more seasoned Harbhajan Singh. This decision was based on instinct, analysis, and an understanding of the situation. Sharma held his nerve, and India won the World Cup.

Corporate Parallel: Business leaders often face similar high-pressure situations. When Steve Jobs decided to remove the physical keyboard from the iPhone, many thought it was a mistake. However, his vision for touchscreen technology paid off and revolutionized the smartphone industry.

2. Adapting Strategies When the Plan Fails

Cricket Example: Ben Stokes' Adjustment in the 2019 World Cup Final

In the 2019 World Cup final, Ben Stokes adapted his approach when England found themselves in deep trouble. Instead of playing aggressively, he switched to a more cautious, calculated approach, guiding England to victory through resilience and adaptability.

Corporate Parallel: When Netflix transitioned from DVD rentals to streaming, it was a huge risk. Had they not adapted their business model, they would have struggled to survive against digital competitors.

3. Taking Accountability for Tough Decisions

Cricket Example: Sourav Ganguly's Decision to Drop Veterans and Back Young Talent

As India's captain, Sourav Ganguly made the tough call to transition from relying on senior players to backing young talents like Yuvraj Singh and Virender Sehwag. This decision was met with criticism initially but proved to be one of the best moves for Indian cricket's future success.

Corporate Parallel: In the corporate world, leaders sometimes have to make difficult personnel decisions. When Satya Nadella became CEO of Microsoft, he shifted the company's focus towards cloud computing, which meant restructuring teams and changing priorities. It was a difficult transition, but it helped Microsoft regain its position as an industry leader.

4. Risk vs. Reward – Calculated Decision-Making

Cricket Example: Eoin Morgan's Aggressive Approach in the 2019 World Cup

Under Eoin Morgan's leadership, England adopted an aggressive batting approach, taking calculated risks in every match. This was a bold strategy, but it paid off, helping England win their first-ever World Cup.

Corporate Parallel: Elon Musk's decision to invest heavily in Tesla's electric vehicle technology at a time when the market was uncertain was a similar high-risk move. Today, Tesla dominates the EV industry, proving that calculated risks can lead to game-changing success.

5. Staying Composed During Crisis Situations

Cricket Example: Rahul Dravid's Leadership in Test Matches

Known as "The Wall," Rahul Dravid was famous for his ability to stay calm and guide his team during crisis situations. His leadership during India's overseas Test victories in difficult conditions showcased resilience and level-headedness under extreme pressure.

Corporate Parallel: A CEO facing economic downturns, like how Howard Schultz managed Starbucks' turnaround during the 2008 financial crisis, requires the same calm approach. He refocused on core values, made strategic changes, and brought the company back to profitability.

Key Takeaways for Corporate Leaders:

- Trust Your Instincts - Experience and data help make better decisions in high-pressure situations.
- Adapt When Plans Fail - Leaders must pivot when circumstances change unexpectedly.
- Take Accountability - Tough decisions require responsibility and confidence.
- Balance Risk and Reward - Calculated risks can lead to massive success.
- Stay Composed Under Pressure - Remaining calm helps navigate crises effectively.

Decision-Making in Cricket and Business

Making tough calls under pressure is what defines great leaders—whether on the cricket field or in the corporate boardroom. Captains like Dhoni, Morgan, and Dravid showcase the importance of calculated risks, adaptability, and staying composed under extreme stress. Similarly, business leaders like Steve Jobs, Elon Musk, and Satya Nadella have all faced critical moments where their decisions shaped the future of their companies.

Understanding the principles of decision-making in cricket can help corporate professionals develop a mindset that embraces pressure, trusts instincts, and makes impactful choices. Just as a great captain steers their team toward victory, a strong corporate leader drives their organization toward sustained success.

Keeping the Team Motivated and Confident

Management Lesson: A motivated and confident team performs better, remains resilient under pressure, and drives long-term success.

In cricket, motivation is as important as skill. A team that believes in itself can overcome challenges, turn matches around, and achieve seemingly impossible victories. Similarly, in business, a motivated workforce drives innovation, productivity, and long-term success.

1. Instilling a Winning Mentality

Cricket Example: Ben Stokes' Heroics in the 2019 Ashes During the third Ashes Test in 2019, Ben Stokes single-handedly led England to an incredible victory with an unbeaten 135. His self-belief and relentless determination not only won the match but also inspired his teammates to believe that no situation is impossible to overcome.

Corporate Parallel: Business leaders must inspire a never-give-up attitude in their teams. Howard Schultz, the former CEO of Starbucks, reinstated confidence in the company when it was struggling, reinforcing a winning mentality that led to its revival.

2. Encouraging Team Bonding and Unity

Cricket Example: New Zealand's Team Culture Under Kane Williamson has been instrumental in fostering an inclusive and cohesive environment within the New Zealand cricket team.

His calm demeanor and emphasis on collective success over individual glory have helped create a unit that thrives under pressure.

Corporate Parallel: Corporate leaders who build a culture of collaboration and teamwork, like Tony Hsieh at Zappos, create work environments where employees feel a sense of belonging, leading to increased productivity and job satisfaction.

3. Handling Failures Positively

- **Cricket Example:** Sachin Tendulkar's Resilience After the 2007 World Cup Exit After India's early exit from the 2007 World Cup, Tendulkar faced immense criticism. However, he used that setback as motivation, working harder on his game and leading India to victory in the 2011 World Cup.
- **Corporate Parallel:** Leaders must treat failures as stepping stones to success. Richard Branson of Virgin Group openly embraces failure, viewing it as an opportunity to innovate and improve.

4. Recognizing and Rewarding Contributions

- Cricket Example: Rohit Sharma's Support for Mumbai Indians' Emerging Players As Mumbai Indians' captain, Rohit Sharma consistently backs young players, giving them the confidence to perform. Players like Hardik Pandya and Jasprit Bumrah flourished under his leadership.
- Corporate Parallel: In business, recognizing contributions boosts morale and motivation. Companies like Netflix empower employees with appreciation-based incentives that reinforce a positive work culture.

5. Maintaining a Positive Environment Under Pressure

- **Cricket Example: Clive Lloyd's Leadership of the Dominant West Indies Team** Under Lloyd's leadership, the West Indies cricket team of the 1970s and 80s became one of the most dominant teams in history. His calm leadership and ability to keep the dressing room motivated created a winning mindset.

- **Corporate Parallel:** Leaders like Satya Nadella at Microsoft have transformed corporate culture by fostering resilience and innovation under pressure, ensuring teams stay focused and motivated even during challenging times.

Key Takeaways for Corporate Leaders:

- **Instill Confidence:** Inspire a winning mentality by leading with belief.
- **Encourage Team Bonding:** A united team performs better and remains motivated.
- **Handle Failures Positively:** Treat setbacks as stepping stones to success.
- **Recognize Contributions:** Celebrating small wins keeps morale high.
- **Maintain a Positive Environment:** Foster a culture of encouragement and support.

Motivation as the Key to Success in Cricket and Business

Cricket captains and corporate leaders share a common goal: to keep their teams motivated and driven toward success. Whether it's Stokes' heroics, Williamson's calm leadership, or Lloyd's team-building, cricket provides invaluable lessons in leadership.

By applying these principles, corporate leaders can create a work environment that fuels passion, nurtures talent, and leads to long-term success—just as great cricket captains do on the field.

Chapter 3

TEAM COORDINATION & ROLE CLARITY

Management Lesson: Clearly defined roles and seamless coordination lead to efficient teamwork and peak performance.

In both cricket and corporate environments, success depends on each individual understanding their responsibilities and working in harmony with the team. Lack of coordination or role clarity can lead to chaos, inefficiencies, and failure.

1. The Importance of Defined Roles

Cricket Example: Rahul Dravid and Virender Sehwag's Contrasting Batting Styles

Dravid, known as "The Wall," played a defensive, steadying role, ensuring stability in the batting lineup. Sehwag, on the other hand, was an aggressive opener who took calculated risks to put the opposition under pressure. Both players had well-defined roles, and their contrasting styles complemented each other, leading to multiple Test victories for India.

Corporate Parallel: In business, different departments serve distinct purposes—finance ensures stability, while marketing drives aggressive outreach. Leaders must define clear roles so that every team member knows their responsibilities and how they contribute to the bigger picture.

2. Effective Coordination Leads to Success

Cricket Example: The Success of Australia's World Cup-Winning Teams

Australia dominated world cricket for decades because of their seamless coordination between batsmen, bowlers, and fielders. Whether it was Glenn McGrath's precision bowling, Adam Gilchrist's aggressive batting, or Ricky Ponting's sharp captaincy, every player functioned like a well-oiled machine, ensuring collective success.

Corporate Parallel: Corporate teams function best when departments work in sync. Just as Australia's team succeeded through disciplined coordination, companies like Apple and Amazon thrive because their R&D, marketing, and supply chain teams operate with efficiency and alignment.

3. Adaptability Within Role Clarity

Cricket Example: Ben Stokes' Versatility as an All-Rounder

Stokes has played different roles based on team needs—aggressive batsman, steady anchor, reliable bowler, and inspirational leader. His ability to adapt while maintaining clarity in his responsibilities makes him invaluable.

Corporate Parallel: Employees must be flexible while maintaining their core responsibilities. In corporate settings, managers who can lead projects, handle crises, and take on new challenges bring immense value to an organization.

4. Trust and Delegation in Team Coordination

Cricket Example: Rohit Sharma's Tactical Captaincy in IPL

Rohit Sharma's success with the Mumbai Indians in the IPL is largely due to his ability to trust his teammates. He assigns roles strategically—giving Jasprit Bumrah the final overs to defend a total or relying on Kieron Pollard's big-hitting during chases.

Corporate Parallel: Great managers delegate tasks to employees based on their strengths. Just as a cricket captain trusts bowlers with match-defining moments, corporate leaders must trust their employees to take ownership of projects and execute them effectively.

5. Handling Conflicts and Avoiding Role Overlaps

Cricket Example: The Clash Between Kevin Pietersen and England's Management

A lack of clarity in leadership roles led to internal conflicts between Kevin Pietersen and England's management. Misunderstandings about his influence on the team dynamic caused disruption and affected England's overall performance.

Corporate Parallel: Role conflicts and unclear authority lines can cause friction in organizations. A structured hierarchy and clear communication prevent overlaps in responsibilities and ensure smooth operations.

Key Takeaways for Corporate Leaders:

- **Define Roles Clearly:** Every team member should understand their responsibilities.
- **Foster Coordination:** Seamless collaboration ensures efficiency and success.
- **Encourage Adaptability:** Employees should be flexible while excelling in core roles.
- **Delegate and Trust:** Leaders should assign responsibilities strategically.
- **Manage Conflicts Effectively:** Clear role demarcation prevents unnecessary disputes.

The Power of Role Clarity and Coordination

Cricket teams and corporate organizations alike thrive when players and employees understand their roles and execute them with precision. From Dravid and Sehwag's contrasting yet complementary roles to Australia's coordinated dominance, cricket offers compelling lessons on structured teamwork.

By adopting these principles, corporate leaders can ensure that their organizations function like well-balanced teams, maximizing efficiency and achieving collective success.

Understanding Individual Strengths

Management Lesson: Leveraging individual talents leads to team success.

A successful team, whether in cricket or business, is built on recognizing and utilizing each member's unique strengths. Understanding the capabilities of each individual allows leaders to place them in roles where they can thrive, contributing to overall success.

1. Identifying Strengths and Assigning Roles

Cricket Example: MS Dhoni Utilizing Players Effectively

Dhoni had a remarkable ability to identify his players' strengths and assign them roles that suited them best. He promoted Rohit Sharma as an opener in limited-overs cricket, a decision that transformed Rohit into one of the world's leading batsmen.

Corporate Parallel: Successful business leaders place employees in roles where they can maximize their potential. Steve Jobs recognized the innovative genius of Jony Ive and gave him creative control over Apple's product design, leading to revolutionary products like the iPhone and MacBook.

2. Balancing Specialization and Versatility

Cricket Example: Jacques Kallis – The Ultimate All-Rounder

Kallis was an all-rounder who excelled in both batting and bowling. His ability to contribute in multiple areas made him invaluable to the South African team.

Corporate Parallel: Employees who can adapt to different roles while specializing in their core strengths add immense value. Elon Musk's leadership across Tesla, SpaceX, and Neuralink highlights the power of balancing specialization with versatility.

3. Building Complementary Partnerships

Cricket Example: The Dravid-Laxman Partnership

Rahul Dravid and VVS Laxman had different playing styles but complemented each other perfectly, rescuing India in tough Test matches, notably the famous 2001 Kolkata Test against Australia.

Corporate Parallel: In business, successful partnerships between product development and marketing teams ensure that innovations reach the right audience. The collaboration between Bill Gates (Microsoft's technology mastermind) and Steve Ballmer (business strategist) helped Microsoft become a tech giant.

4. Encouraging Players to Play to Their Strengths

Cricket Example: Virender Sehwag's Free-Flowing Batting

Despite criticism for his unconventional technique, Sehwag stuck to his aggressive batting style, which made him one of India's most successful openers.

Corporate Parallel: Business leaders should encourage employees to use their unique skills rather than forcing them into rigid molds. Richard Branson of Virgin Group fosters an environment where employees are encouraged to be creative and take risks.

5. Recognizing and Developing Potential

Cricket Example: Sourav Ganguly Backing Young Players

Ganguly identified and backed future stars like Yuvraj Singh, Harbhajan Singh, and Virender Sehwag, helping them develop into match-winners.

Corporate Parallel: Great leaders mentor and nurture talent within organizations. Google's leadership ensures continuous learning and skill development among employees, leading to sustained innovation.

Key Takeaways for Corporate Leaders:

- **Identify Strengths:** Assign roles based on individual capabilities.
- **Balance Specialization and Versatility:** Encourage skill diversity while maintaining focus.
- **Build Complementary Partnerships:** Pair employees whose skills complement each other.
- **Encourage Unique Talents:** Let employees play to their strengths for optimal performance.
- **Develop Future Leaders:** Invest in mentoring and upskilling talent.

Leveraging Strengths for Team Success

Cricket and corporate management both emphasize the importance of recognizing and utilizing individual strengths. Whether it's Dhoni backing Rohit Sharma, Dravid and Laxman's partnership, or business leaders placing employees in roles where they excel, success comes from understanding and leveraging talent effectively.

By applying these principles, corporate leaders can build high-performing teams, unlock innovation, and drive long-term success—just as great cricket teams do on the field.

Trusting Teammates to Do Their Job

Management Lesson: Trusting team members empowers them to perform at their best, enhances efficiency, and strengthens overall team success.

Trust is the foundation of any high-performing team. Whether in cricket or corporate management, trusting teammates to execute their responsibilities allows a team to function smoothly and perform under pressure. Leaders who delegate and trust their team members create an environment of accountability and confidence.

1. Trust in Leadership and Execution

Cricket Example: Kapil Dev's Trust in His Team – 1983 World Cup Final

In the 1983 World Cup final, India faced a formidable West Indies team. After scoring a modest 183, the odds were stacked against India. However, Kapil Dev trusted his bowlers to execute their skills and backed them completely. His trust paid off as Mohinder Amarnath and Madan Lal stepped up to bowl India to a historic victory.

Corporate Parallel: Business leaders must trust their employees to make critical decisions. When Warren Buffett invests in companies, he trusts the leadership teams to execute their vision without interference, ensuring a decentralized and empowered management system.

2. Delegating Key Responsibilities

Cricket Example: MS Dhoni's Faith in Joginder Sharma – 2007 T20 World Cup Final

Dhoni made a surprising decision to let an inexperienced Joginder Sharma bowl the final over of the 2007 T20 World Cup final instead of opting for a senior bowler. His trust in Sharma's ability to hold his nerve under pressure paid off, and India won the title.

Corporate Parallel: A CEO who delegates responsibilities to emerging leaders allows them to grow. Steve Jobs trusted Tim

Cook to handle Apple's supply chain before eventually making him CEO, proving the importance of delegation in long-term success.

3. Encouraging Team Members to Take Ownership

Cricket Example: Eoin Morgan's Captaincy in the 2019 World Cup

Morgan created a culture where players were given the freedom to express themselves. By trusting his players, such as Ben Stokes in the final, Morgan allowed them to make match-winning decisions under pressure.

Corporate Parallel: Leaders at companies like Google allow employees to experiment with innovative ideas through initiatives like Google's 20% time policy, where employees work on projects of their choosing.

4. Trust Fosters Innovation and Risk-Taking

As head coach of India's U-19 and India A teams, Dravid trusted young cricketers like Shubman Gill and Prithvi Shaw to take risks and express themselves on the field, preparing them for international success.

Corporate Parallel: Amazon fosters a culture of innovation by allowing employees to experiment with bold ideas, leading to the success of services like AWS and Prime.

Key Takeaways for Corporate Leaders:

- **Empower Team Members:** Trusting employees leads to better decision-making and accountability.
- **Delegate Responsibilities:** Leaders must allow emerging talent to handle key roles.
- **Encourage Ownership:** Give team members the freedom to take responsibility for outcomes.
- **Support Teammates in Pressure Situations:** Show confidence in their abilities.
- **Foster a Culture of Trust:** Teams that trust each other perform better in high-pressure environments.

The Power of Trust in Teams

Whether in the 1983 World Cup, Dhoni's leadership, or corporate success stories, trust is the foundation of high-performing teams. Leaders who empower and believe in their teams create an environment of confidence, accountability, and excellence.

By applying these principles, corporate leaders can build teams that thrive under pressure and drive sustained success—just as great cricket teams do on the field.

Importance of Role Allocation

Management Lesson: Assigning the right roles to the right individuals maximizes team efficiency and success.

In both cricket and corporate settings, role allocation is a crucial aspect of success. When players or employees are assigned tasks that align with their strengths, the overall team functions more effectively. Properly defined roles eliminate confusion, improve performance, and create an environment where individuals can thrive in their respective areas.

1. Role Allocation Revolutionizing Strategy

Cricket Example: Sanath Jayasuriya & Romesh Kaluwitharana's Explosive Opening Partnership – 1996 World Cup

Before the 1996 World Cup, opening batsmen were typically expected to play cautiously. However, Sri Lanka's coach and captain assigned the aggressive Kaluwitharana and Jayasuriya as openers, revolutionizing limited-overs cricket with their attacking style. Their explosive starts changed the dynamics of one-day cricket, leading Sri Lanka to their maiden World Cup victory.

Corporate Parallel: In business, strategic role allocation can disrupt an industry. Netflix moved key executives into content production roles, leading to its dominance in streaming services. Identifying the right personnel for key roles is essential in staying ahead in a competitive environment.

2. Balancing Experience and Fresh Talent

Cricket Example: England's Test Team Transition Under Joe Root

When Joe Root led England, he balanced experienced players like James Anderson with young talents like Ollie Pope and Zak Crawley. By strategically allocating roles based on skills and experience, England ensured stability while fostering future talent.

Corporate Parallel: Successful companies balance senior executives' experience with fresh talent's innovative ideas. Companies like Google and Tesla place young leaders in research and development roles while maintaining experienced professionals in leadership positions.

3. The Right Player for the Right Job

Cricket Example: Rahul Tewatia's Role as a Finisher in the IPL

Rahul Tewatia was not a marquee player, but the Rajasthan Royals assigned him the role of a finisher in crucial matches. His ability to handle pressure helped his team secure incredible wins, including his famous five-sixes-over performance.

Corporate Parallel: Assigning employees to roles where they can perform under pressure ensures business success. Amazon's logistics team identifies high-pressure problem solvers for handling supply chain disruptions.

4. Specialization for Maximum Impact

Cricket Example: Lasith Malinga as a Death-Over Specialist

Malinga wasn't just a fast bowler; he was assigned the role of a death-over specialist, which allowed him to focus on perfecting yorkers. His impact won crucial matches for Sri Lanka and the Mumbai Indians in high-pressure situations.

Corporate Parallel: Companies assign specialists to key areas—Apple's industrial designers focus purely on product aesthetics while software engineers specialize in user interface development, ensuring quality in every domain.

Key Takeaways for Corporate Leaders:

- **Identify Strengths Early:** Assign roles that align with each team member's capabilities.
- **Balance Experience and Fresh Perspectives:** A mix of seasoned professionals and young innovators leads to success.
- **Define Roles Clearly:** Eliminate confusion to enhance productivity.
- **Encourage Specialization:** Allow individuals to focus on their areas of expertise.
- **Adapt When Necessary:** Be flexible in reallocating roles based on evolving situations.

The Power of Role Allocation

Whether it's Jayasuriya and Kaluwitharana redefining opening partnerships or businesses like Netflix strategically placing leaders in new roles, proper role allocation is key to sustained success. In both cricket and corporate management, identifying, assigning, and adjusting roles based on individual strengths leads to peak performance and long-term success.

Chapter 4

DELEGATION: TRUSTING YOUR TEAM

Management Lesson: Delegating responsibilities empowers team members, enhances efficiency, and fosters leadership development.

Delegation is a crucial leadership skill that allows teams to function effectively. In cricket, a captain cannot win a match alone—every player has a role to play, and trusting teammates to execute their responsibilities leads to success. Similarly, in business, leaders who delegate responsibilities create an environment where employees feel empowered, motivated, and accountable.

1. Delegating Key Responsibilities in High-Stakes Situations

Cricket Example: MS Dhoni Entrusting Joginder Sharma in the 2007 T20 World Cup Final

In a high-pressure moment, Dhoni gave the final over of the T20 World Cup final to an inexperienced Joginder Sharma instead of a seasoned bowler. This decision reflected Dhoni's trust in his player, and Sharma delivered by securing the trophy for India.

Corporate Parallel: A CEO trusting a young leader to spearhead an important project can lead to unexpected success. Sundar Pichai was entrusted with leading Google Chrome before rising to the role of CEO, demonstrating the power of delegation.

2. Empowering Emerging Talent

Cricket Example: Kane Williamson's Trust in Young Players

As New Zealand's captain, Williamson has consistently backed young players like Devon Conway and Kyle Jamieson, giving them opportunities to shine on the international stage.

Corporate Parallel: Companies like Amazon and Microsoft delegate key projects to emerging leaders, ensuring they gain experience while also driving innovation.

3. Balancing Micromanagement vs. Trust

Cricket Example: Eoin Morgan's Approach in the 2019 World Cup

Morgan allowed his players to take ownership of their roles, trusting them to execute aggressive strategies. His hands-off approach and confidence in his team created a fearless environment that led England to their first-ever World Cup victory.

Corporate Parallel: In business, leaders who micromanage limit creativity and efficiency. A great example is Elon Musk, who delegates execution to department heads while focusing on vision and strategy.

4. Creating Future Leaders

Cricket Example: Rohit Sharma Grooming Leadership in Mumbai Indians

Rohit has developed young players like Hardik Pandya and Jasprit Bumrah by trusting them in crucial match situations, preparing them for leadership roles in Indian cricket.

Corporate Parallel: Organizations that groom future leaders through delegation build long-term success. Companies like Apple and Tesla strategically assign leadership projects to identify and develop the next generation of executives.

Key Takeaways for Corporate Leaders:

- **Empower Through Trust:** Give employees responsibilities to build confidence and efficiency.
- **Encourage Leadership Development:** Delegation fosters future leaders within the organization.
- **Avoid Micromanagement:** Trust team members to execute tasks without excessive interference.
- **Support Decision-Making:** Back employees, even when they take calculated risks.
- **Balance Responsibilities:** Assign roles strategically to optimize performance.

The Power of Delegation

Just as captains like Dhoni, Morgan, and Rohit Sharma trust their players to deliver, business leaders must delegate effectively to empower their teams. Delegation fosters trust, boosts efficiency, and grooms the next generation of leaders.

By applying these principles, corporate leaders can ensure their organizations function seamlessly, innovate consistently, and achieve long-term success—just like a well-balanced cricket team on the field.

Why Micro-Management Fails

Management Lesson: Over-controlling stifles creativity, lowers confidence, and reduces efficiency.

Micro-management—where leaders excessively control and oversee tasks—can be detrimental to a team's success. In cricket, captains who fail to trust their players and constantly interfere with their approach end up damaging morale and performance. In business, managers who micromanage their teams create an environment of stress, reducing productivity and innovation.

1. Over-Controlling Limits Creativity

Cricket Example: England's Struggles Before Eoin Morgan's Captaincy

Before Eoin Morgan took charge, England's white-ball strategy was rigid, with players unable to express themselves freely. Micro-management by previous leadership led to a defensive mindset, preventing England from evolving with modern cricket. Morgan's leadership removed excessive control, allowing players to play aggressive cricket, leading to England's 2019 World Cup victory.

Corporate Parallel: Companies that impose excessive reporting and rigid work flows limit employees' ability to think creatively. Netflix's success is attributed to a culture of trust, where employees are given autonomy rather than being micro-managed.

2. Trusting Players Enhances Performance

Cricket Example: Pat Cummins' Leadership for Australia

Unlike past Australian captains who enforced strict structures, Cummins allows players to take ownership of their roles. His relaxed, trust-driven approach has led to more natural performances, evident in Australia's recent Test dominance.

Corporate Parallel: Google's innovative products come from a leadership culture that trusts employees to work independently.

Over-management would stifle innovation and creativity.

3. Players Must Make Their Own Decisions in Pressure Situations

Cricket Example: Hardik Pandya's Captaincy in IPL

When leading Gujarat Titans in the IPL, Pandya gave responsibility to his bowlers, allowing them to set their fields and execute strategies. This freedom allowed players like Rashid Khan to thrive under pressure.

Corporate Parallel: Successful businesses empower employees to make critical decisions. Tesla's leadership philosophy allows employees to take ownership of projects, reducing reliance on senior oversight.

4. Micromanagement Slows Decision-Making

Cricket Example: Virat Kohli's Aggressive Leadership vs. Rigid Approaches

Kohli's leadership allowed bowlers like Mohammed Shami and Jasprit Bumrah to take charge of their strategies instead of over-relying on instructions. This approach led to quick decision-making under pressure.

Corporate Parallel: Companies with multiple approval layers slow decision-making. Startups like SpaceX thrive by allowing quick, decentralized decision-making, reducing bureaucracy.

Key Takeaways for Corporate Leaders:

- **Give Teams Freedom:** Trust team members to execute tasks without excessive control.
- **Encourage Independent Thinking:** Allow players/ employees to innovate and make their own decisions.
- **Reduce Over-Management:** Avoid unnecessary supervision that slows processes.
- **Focus on Strategy, Not Small Tasks:** Leaders should set the vision but let teams execute.
- **Foster Confidence in the Team:** Players and employees perform best when they feel trusted.

Letting Go for Greater Success

Cricket captains like Morgan, Cummins, and Pandya have shown that empowering teams leads to success. Similarly, corporate leaders must trust their teams, delegate effectively, and focus on strategic vision rather than micro-managing.

By applying these lessons, business leaders can create environments where innovation, accountability, and efficiency thrive—just as great cricket teams do on the field.

Identifying Key Players for Crucial Situations

Management Lesson: Recognizing and utilizing the right individuals at the right time is crucial for success.

Every team has players who thrive under pressure. The ability to identify these players and assign them key roles during defining moments determines the success of a cricket team or a corporate organization. Effective leaders know when to turn to their best performers and how to position them for maximum impact.

1. Trusting a Reliable Anchor

Cricket Example: Sunil Gavaskar's Role in Test Cricket

Gavaskar was India's go-to batsman in tough Test matches. His ability to bat for long hours and build an innings made him the perfect player to anchor the team in challenging conditions.

Corporate Parallel: In business, reliable leaders are needed to steer a company during crises. Tim Cook took over Apple's leadership after Steve Jobs, maintaining stability and ensuring smooth operations during a crucial transition phase.

2. Game-Changers in High-Stakes Moments

Cricket Example: Vivian Richards' Impact in Big Matches

Richards was the ultimate match-winner for the West Indies. His aggressive batting in pressure situations, like the 1979 World Cup final, showcased his ability to turn games around.

Corporate Parallel: In corporate settings, certain individuals drive change. Elon Musk, for example, is known for taking risks and making bold moves that redefine industries, much like Richards' dominance in cricket.

3. Identifying Emerging Stars

Cricket Example: India Betting on Yashasvi Jaiswal in Test Cricket

Jaiswal's rise in the Indian Test team showcases the importance of identifying and nurturing young talent for future success.

Corporate Parallel: Startups often rely on young innovators to disrupt industries. Mark Zuckerberg recognized Sheryl Sandberg's leadership potential early on, making her a key figure in Facebook's expansion.

Empowering Team Members with Responsibilities

Management Lesson: Giving team members responsibility enhances confidence, accountability, and performance.

A successful team is built on trust. Leaders must delegate tasks and give players and employees the freedom to execute their roles confidently. Empowering individuals fosters a sense of ownership and accountability, leading to higher performance levels.

1. Backing Players to Perform

Cricket Example: Kapil Dev Leading a Young Indian Team in 1983

Kapil Dev trusted his team despite their inexperience, giving players like Mohinder Amarnath and Madan Lal key roles in crucial situations. His faith resulted in India's first World Cup triumph.

Corporate Parallel: Startups empower employees by giving them leadership responsibilities early. Companies like Tesla and Google encourage employees to take ownership of projects, leading to innovative breakthroughs.

2. Trusting All-Rounders to Deliver

Cricket Example: Ben Stokes' Role in England's 2019 World Cup

Stokes was trusted as England's go-to player in crucial situations. His all-round capabilities allowed him to influence matches with both bat and ball.

Corporate Parallel: Businesses rely on multi-skilled employees to drive growth. Leaders like Satya Nadella at Microsoft empower cross-functional teams to take charge of major projects.

3. Handing Over Leadership to Future Generations

Cricket Example: Ricky Ponting Grooming Michael Clarke

Ponting played a key role in mentoring Clarke, who later took over the Australian captaincy and led the team to success.

Corporate Parallel: In corporate environments, succession planning is critical. Amazon's Jeff Bezos prepared Andy Jassy to take over as CEO, ensuring a smooth transition and continued growth.

Key Takeaways for Corporate Leaders:

- **Recognize Key Performers:** Identify individuals who excel under pressure.
- **Empower Future Leaders:** Allow emerging talent to take on responsibilities.
- **Delegate Important Tasks:** Trust employees to execute their roles.
- **Provide Leadership Opportunities:** Groom the next generation of decision-makers.
- **Create a Culture of Trust:** Employees perform best when they feel valued and empowered.

The Role of Trust and Recognition in Success

Whether in cricket or corporate management, identifying key players and empowering them is essential for success. Legends like Gavaskar, Richards, and Kapil Dev thrived because they were entrusted with responsibilities that suited their strengths.

By applying these lessons, corporate leaders can build high-performing teams that operate efficiently, innovate continuously, and succeed under pressure—just like a champion cricket team.

Chapter 5

COMMUNICATION: THE WINNING CONVERSATION

Management Lesson: Effective communication builds trust, strengthens coordination, and enhances performance.

Great teams, whether in cricket or business, thrive on strong communication. Clear, timely, and effective communication ensures that strategies are understood, roles are well-defined, and team members remain aligned toward a common goal. Without it, confusion can lead to poor execution and missed opportunities.

1. On-Field Communication for Success

Cricket Example: Ben Stokes & Jos Buttler in the 2019 World Cup Final

During the high-pressure Super Over of the 2019 World Cup final, Stokes and Buttler maintained constant communication, discussing each shot, adjusting their running, and ensuring they maximized every scoring opportunity. Their clear conversations helped England secure their maiden World Cup.

Corporate Parallel: In a corporate setting, teams working on tight deadlines must have seamless communication to execute projects efficiently. Apple's design and engineering teams constantly communicate during product development, ensuring the final product meets market expectations.

2. Captain-to-Player Conversations

Cricket Example: Kane Williamson's Approach with Young Players

Williamson, as New Zealand's captain, is known for his calm and composed conversations with young players. His ability to communicate tactical adjustments and encouragement ensures that inexperienced players feel supported and perform at their best.

Corporate Parallel: In the workplace, senior executives must mentor young employees through effective communication. Google's leadership fosters open dialogue, where junior employees can voice ideas without hesitation.

3. Bowling Strategies & Field Placements

Cricket Example: Ravichandran Ashwin & Virat Kohli's Tactical Conversations

Ashwin and Kohli are often seen discussing field placements before crucial overs. Their strategic communication helps plan how to dismiss opposition batsmen based on weaknesses and match conditions.

Corporate Parallel: Project managers must collaborate with team members, adjusting strategies based on client feedback and market shifts, just as captains adjust bowling tactics based on the game situation.

4. Handling Tough Situations Through Effective Communication

Cricket Example: Rahul Dravid's Mentorship in Indian Cricket

Dravid, as India's coach and mentor, has been instrumental in shaping young players by engaging in one-on-one conversations to help them handle pressure situations.

Corporate Parallel: In business, leaders must communicate calmly in crises. During Tesla's early struggles, Elon Musk reassured employees with clear, strategic guidance, helping the company stay focused and resilient.

Key Takeaways for Corporate Leaders:

- **Encourage Open Dialogue:** Ensure employees feel comfortable sharing ideas and concerns.
- **Communicate Under Pressure:** Clear messaging during high-stakes moments leads to better decision-making.
- **Strategic Discussions Improve Execution:** Tactical conversations help align teams toward common goals.
- **Mentorship Strengthens Teams:** Providing guidance through effective communication builds confidence in young talent.
- **Collaboration Fosters Success:** Strong communication between departments enhances overall performance.

The Power of Communication in Leadership

Effective communication in cricket and corporate management ensures clarity, fosters trust, and enhances team performance. Whether it's Stokes and Buttler planning in a Super Over, Williamson guiding young players, or Dravid mentoring future stars, the ability to communicate clearly and efficiently separates great leaders from the rest.

By applying these lessons, corporate leaders can build high-performing teams, drive innovation, and achieve long-term success—just like champion cricket teams on the field.

The Importance of Non-Verbal Cues and Signals

Management Lesson: Silent communication can be just as powerful as spoken words, fostering trust and efficiency.

In both cricket and corporate settings, non-verbal communication plays a crucial role in ensuring seamless coordination. Body language, eye contact, hand signals, and even facial expressions can convey critical messages without disrupting focus.

1. Silent Coordination in Pressure Moments

Cricket Example: MS Dhoni's Subtle Signals to Bowlers

Dhoni was known for guiding his bowlers through subtle glances, nods, and hand gestures rather than excessive verbal instructions. Whether it was setting the field or advising a bowler about where to pitch the ball, Dhoni's calm yet precise signals ensured his team executed plans without hesitation.

Corporate Parallel: In boardrooms, effective leaders use non-verbal cues such as eye contact, posture, and facial expressions to guide discussions and convey authority without interrupting team flow.

2. Understanding Teammates Without Words

Cricket Example: Virat Kohli & AB de Villiers' Running Between the Wickets

Kohli and de Villiers formed a deadly duo for Royal Challengers Bangalore. Their ability to communicate through quick glances and body movements while running between the wickets made them one of the best pairs in IPL history.

Corporate Parallel: In a corporate environment, seamless teamwork is essential. Software development teams at companies like Google and Apple rely on minimal verbal communication, using dashboards, gestures, and concise signals to stay aligned.

How Captains Communicate Strategies in Crunch Moments

Management Lesson: The best leaders deliver concise, clear messages in high-pressure situations to maintain team focus.

Captains in cricket, much like corporate leaders, must convey complex strategies in high-pressure moments without overwhelming their teams. Great captains use concise, impactful communication to ensure the team stays focused and confident.

1. Making Tactical Adjustments in the Heat of Battle

Cricket Example: Ben Stokes' On-Field Instructions in the 2019 World Cup Final

Stokes constantly communicated with bowlers and fielders during the dramatic Super Over, ensuring England remained sharp under pressure. His ability to simplify instructions and maintain composure helped England secure their first-ever ODI World Cup win.

Corporate Parallel: In corporate settings, leaders must make quick, strategic pivots when unexpected challenges arise. During a product launch crisis, leaders at Tesla and SpaceX adjust plans with clear, direct communication, ensuring teams remain aligned.

2. Motivating the Team in High-Pressure Moments

Cricket Example: Imran Khan's 'Cornered Tigers' Speech in the 1992 World Cup

Before Pakistan's crucial matches in the 1992 World Cup, Imran Khan inspired his team by calling them "cornered tigers." His powerful words instilled belief, and Pakistan went on to win their first World Cup.

Corporate Parallel: CEOs like Steve Jobs were known for rallying their teams before product launches, using compelling speeches to create a sense of mission and urgency.

Feedback & Constructive Criticism in Corporate Settings

Management Lesson: Providing feedback in the right manner helps individuals grow and improves team performance.

Great teams in both cricket and corporate settings thrive on continuous learning. Constructive criticism, when delivered effectively, helps individuals and teams refine their strategies and improve their performance.

1. Constructive Criticism Fosters Growth

Cricket Example: Rahul Dravid's Mentorship at the NCA

As head of India's National Cricket Academy, Dravid provides honest, constructive feedback to young players, helping them refine their techniques and mental approach.

Corporate Parallel: Successful companies like Amazon and Microsoft emphasize continuous learning by encouraging leaders to provide direct but supportive feedback that enhances team performance.

2. Post-Match Reviews and Learning from Mistakes

Cricket Example: Ricky Ponting's Analytical Approach

Ponting was known for conducting in-depth post-match analysis, identifying what went right and what needed improvement. His ability to assess performances and provide actionable insights made Australia a dominant force in world cricket.

Corporate Parallel: After major project launches, top companies conduct debriefs to analyze outcomes, just as Ponting did after every series to refine strategies for future matches.

Key Takeaways for Corporate Leaders:

- **Leverage Non-Verbal Communication:** Body language and subtle signals can enhance efficiency and trust.
- **Deliver Clear Strategies in Pressure Moments:** Concise messaging ensures alignment under high stakes.
- **Motivate Through Strong Communication:** Words can inspire teams to perform beyond expectations.
- **Provide Constructive Feedback:** A growth mindset is essential for continuous improvement.
- **Analyze Performance for Future Success:** Learning from past mistakes builds a resilient and adaptive team.

Communication as the Backbone of Leadership

From Dhoni's silent signals to Stokes' tactical discussions and Imran Khan's inspiring words, communication in cricket has shaped match-winning moments. In the corporate world, effective communication ensures teams remain aligned, motivated, and adaptable in high-pressure situations.

By applying these lessons, corporate leaders can create environments where clear messaging, trust, and constructive feedback drive their teams to success—just like great cricket captains leading their teams on the field.

Chapter 6

DECISION-MAKING UNDER PRESSURE

Management Lesson: High-pressure situations demand clarity, quick thinking, and trust in one's instincts.

Whether in cricket or business, leaders must make critical decisions in high-stakes moments. The ability to stay composed, assess the situation, and act decisively is what separates great leaders from the rest.

1. Tactical Brilliance in Crunch Situations

Cricket Example: Pat Cummins' Captaincy in the 2023 World Test Championship Final

Pat Cummins displayed exceptional decision-making in the final against India, balancing aggressive bowling changes and field placements. His ability to rotate his bowlers effectively and use short-ball tactics under pressure helped Australia secure the prestigious title.

Corporate Parallel: In the business world, CEOs must make bold strategic moves under pressure. When Apple's Steve Jobs launched the iPhone despite skepticism, his decision revolutionized the tech industry.

2. Trusting Instincts When the Stakes Are High

Cricket Example: Shreyas Iyer's Decision to Attack in IPL 2022

Leading Kolkata Knight Riders, Shreyas Iyer took an aggressive approach in crucial chases, backing his instincts to promote power-hitters at unexpected moments. His risk-taking mindset turned matches in his team's favor.

Corporate Parallel: Business leaders who take calculated risks can achieve breakthroughs. Jeff Bezos' decision to invest in cloud computing (AWS) despite doubts turned Amazon into a tech powerhouse.

3. Making the Right Bowling Change at the Right Time

Cricket Example: Ben Stokes' Leadership in the 2022 T20 World Cup Final

Stokes, known for thriving under pressure, strategically changed bowlers at key moments in the final against Pakistan. His composed decision-making helped England restrict Pakistan to a manageable total, leading to a historic victory.

Corporate Parallel: In crisis situations, leaders must pivot quickly. Elon Musk's ability to adjust Tesla's supply chain during the global chip shortage kept the company ahead of competitors.

4. Field Placements and Adaptability

Cricket Example: Babar Azam's Captaincy During the 2021 T20 World Cup

Babar Azam's strategic field placements and ability to read the game helped Pakistan defeat India for the first time in a World Cup match. His calculated decisions ensured efficient execution by his bowlers.

Corporate Parallel: Business leaders must adapt to dynamic market conditions. Netflix shifted from DVD rentals to streaming when consumer preferences changed, demonstrating the power of timely decision-making.

5. Handling Pressure in High-Stakes Situations

Cricket Example: Jasprit Bumrah's Super Over Decision-Making

Bumrah's calm under pressure in multiple Super Over situations has made him India's go-to bowler in tight games. His ability to assess the batsman's weakness and adjust his line and length in real-time is a testament to elite decision-making.

Corporate Parallel: In the corporate world, leaders handling mergers and acquisitions must stay composed under pressure. When Satya Nadella led Microsoft's acquisition of Linked In, his strategic vision helped expand the company's professional network reach.

Key Takeaways for Corporate Leaders:

- **Stay Calm Under Pressure:** Composure allows better decision-making in high-stakes moments.
- **Trust Your Instincts:** Experience builds confidence in making quick, strategic decisions.

- **Adapt Strategies as Needed:** Leaders must pivot based on changing situations.
- **Back Your Team's Strengths:** Effective delegation and role clarity lead to success.
- **Think Long-Term:** Decisions should align with broader goals, not just immediate outcomes.

The Power of Decisive Leadership

Great cricket captains and business leaders share a common trait—composure under pressure. Whether it's Cummins making a bold bowling change, Stokes guiding England in a final, or a CEO pivoting a business model, decisive leadership is the key to success.

By applying these principles, corporate leaders can navigate complex challenges, inspire confidence in their teams, and drive sustained success—just as great cricketers do on the field.

Risk-Taking vs. Playing It Safe

Management Lesson: Knowing when to take calculated risks and when to play conservatively is key to long-term success.

In both cricket and business, success often hinges on the ability to assess risk and reward. Leaders must decide whether to take aggressive action or adopt a more measured approach based on the situation at hand.

1. The Balance Between Attack and Defense

Cricket Example: Rishabh Pant's Aggressive Batting in Test Cricket

Rishabh Pant has redefined Test cricket with his fearless approach. His counter-attacking innings in Australia (2021) played a crucial role in India's historic series win. While many would have played cautiously, Pant's calculated aggression shifted momentum in India's favor.

Corporate Parallel: In business, companies like Tesla take bold risks by investing in cutting-edge technology and expanding aggressively, while companies like IBM prefer steady, strategic growth.

2. Playing It Safe When Required

Cricket Example: Kane Williamson's Controlled Approach

Williamson is known for his ability to assess match conditions and play accordingly. In the 2021 World Test Championship final, he anchored New Zealand's chase with a patient 52*, choosing to play safe rather than taking unnecessary risks.

Corporate Parallel: Apple is known for playing safe with product launches, making incremental improvements rather than introducing radical changes. This approach ensures steady growth and reliability.

Learning from Wrong Decisions

Management Lesson: Mistakes are stepping stones to success if analyzed and learned from.

Every leader, in both cricket and business, makes wrong decisions. The ability to acknowledge, learn from, and improve upon mistakes separates the best from the rest.

1. Bouncing Back from Poor Captaincy Calls

Cricket Example: Rohit Sharma's Adjustment as India's Captain

Initially criticized for conservative field placements in Test matches, Rohit Sharma adapted his approach by making more aggressive bowling changes, helping India secure crucial victories in 2023.

Corporate Parallel: Business leaders who acknowledge failures and pivot strategies succeed. Satya Nadella revamped Microsoft's business model after its mobile failure, focusing on cloud computing to drive growth.

2. Learning from Tactical Errors

Cricket Example: Hardik Pandya's Bowling Decision in IPL 2022

As Gujarat Titans' captain, Pandya's initial misjudgments in bowling changes cost his team a few matches. However, he quickly adjusted his strategies, ultimately leading his team to an IPL title in their debut season.

Corporate Parallel: Netflix originally started as a DVD rental service before pivoting to streaming after realizing the shift in consumer behavior. This ability to learn from mistakes transformed the company into an industry leader.

The Ability to Adapt to Unforeseen Challenges

Management Lesson: Success lies in responding quickly to changing circumstances.

Great leaders, whether in cricket or corporate management, must adapt when faced with unexpected situations. Flexibility, quick decision-making, and resilience are essential qualities for sustained success.

1. Adjusting to Changing Match Conditions

Cricket Example: Travis Head's Adaptability in the 2023 World Test Championship Final

Travis Head played an aggressive knock despite tough conditions, adapting his technique to counter the swinging ball. His ability to change his approach mid-match proved crucial in Australia's victory.

Corporate Parallel: Businesses had to adapt quickly to remote work during the COVID-19 pandemic. Companies like Zoom and Slack adjusted their strategies to cater to the sudden demand for virtual collaboration tools.

2. Overcoming Unexpected Setbacks

Cricket Example: Shubman Gill's Role Change in India's Batting Order

Initially an opener, Gill was asked to bat in the middle order during the 2023 ODI World Cup. Instead of struggling, he adapted quickly and delivered match-winning performances.

Corporate Parallel: Startups that pivot based on market demands often find success. Airbnb initially struggled as a rental service but adapted to offer unique travel experiences, becoming a global leader.

Key Takeaways for Corporate Leaders:

- **Assess Risk Wisely:** Knowing when to take risks and when to play it safe is crucial.
- **Learn from Failures:** Mistakes should be seen as learning opportunities, not setbacks.
- **Be Adaptable:** Leaders must adjust strategies to tackle unforeseen challenges.
- **Encourage Bold Thinking:** Teams should be empowered to innovate while balancing risk.
- **Pivot When Necessary:** Business strategies should evolve with market changes.

The Winning Formula in Cricket and Business

The greatest cricketers and business leaders know when to take risks, learn from their mistakes, and adapt to unexpected challenges. Whether it's Pant taking on Australia's bowlers, Williamson playing it safe, or companies like Tesla and Apple making strategic choices, success comes from making the right decisions at the right time.

By applying these lessons, corporate leaders can develop resilience, foster innovation, and navigate uncertain times—just as elite cricketers do on the field.

Chapter 7

TIME MANAGEMENT – MAKING EVERY BALL COUNT

Management Lesson: Utilizing time effectively and making the most of every opportunity is key to success in both cricket and business.

Time is a limited resource in cricket and corporate management. Whether it's managing the 50 overs in an ODI or making split-second decisions in a T20 match, the best players and leaders excel in optimizing time for maximum efficiency.

1. Mastering the Art of Chasing Under Pressure

Cricket Example: Glenn Maxwell's 201-run Knock Against Afghanistan in the 2023 ODI World Cup

In a record-breaking chase, Glenn Maxwell single-handedly took Australia to victory despite suffering cramps. He managed time effectively, pacing his innings with calculated risks before accelerating in the final overs to achieve an improbable win.

Corporate Parallel: Business leaders facing tight deadlines must balance workload distribution, ensuring efficiency without burnout—just like Maxwell managed his energy while executing a historic chase.

2. Accelerating at the Right Time in T20 Cricket

Cricket Example: Suryakumar Yadav's Strike Rate Management in T20 Cricket

Suryakumar Yadav is known for his ability to manage time effectively in T20 matches. Instead of going for big shots from ball one, he assesses conditions and then accelerates when the moment is right, ensuring maximum impact.

Corporate Parallel: In business, knowing when to push aggressively for expansion or play safe is crucial. Startups like Uber initially expanded cautiously before aggressively scaling up when the market was ripe.

3. Time-Conscious Captaincy Decisions

Cricket Example: Jos Buttler's Tactical Captaincy in the 2022 T20 World Cup

As England's white-ball captain, Buttler expertly rotated his bowlers and adjusted field placements quickly, ensuring minimal time wastage and putting pressure on the opposition.

Corporate Parallel: CEOs and project managers must make real-time decisions, optimizing available time to maximize productivity, just as Buttler manages limited overs efficiently.

4. Powerplay Utilization in T20 Cricket

Cricket Example: David Warner's Explosive Starts in Powerplays

Warner consistently capitalizes on the first six overs in T20s, ensuring his team gets a strong foundation, demonstrating how early momentum can shape an entire innings.

Corporate Parallel: Businesses launching new products must capitalize on market trends early, just as Warner capitalizes on field restrictions to maximize scoring opportunities.

5. Adapting Strategies When Time is Running Out

Cricket Example: Ravindra Jadeja's Quick Cameos in Final Overs

Jadeja has mastered the art of finishing innings with quick, calculated shots, knowing that time is limited and maximizing every ball he faces.

Corporate Parallel: Businesses in crisis mode need rapid adaptability—companies like Airbnb pivoted quickly during the COVID-19 pandemic by focusing on local stays instead of global travel, making the most of available opportunities.

Key Takeaways for Corporate Leaders:

- **Prioritize Tasks Wisely:** Focus on what delivers the most value within limited time.
- **Adapt to Changing Situations:** Adjust strategies based on real-time feedback.
- **Know When to Accelerate:** Timing is everything in executing business decisions.
- **Utilize the First-Mover Advantage:** Making an impact early, like capitalizing on powerplays in T20 cricket, ensures long-term success.
- **Optimize Limited Resources:** Whether in the final overs of a match or a project deadline, maximizing impact within constraints is key.

The Power of Time Management in Cricket and Business

Whether it's Maxwell crafting an epic chase, Warner using powerplays, or Buttler managing England's bowling rotations, effective time management is crucial in cricket. In corporate settings, leaders who optimize their schedules, prioritize urgent tasks, and execute strategies at the right time gain a competitive edge.

By applying these principles, corporate professionals can enhance productivity, make informed decisions, and drive long-term success—just as great cricketers make every ball count on the field.

How to Handle Deadlines Under Pressure

Management Lesson: Effective time management and composure under pressure lead to success in crucial moments.

Deadlines in business and final overs in cricket share a common challenge—intense pressure and limited time. The best performers remain calm, assess their options quickly, and execute with precision.

1. Delivering Under Pressure

Cricket Example: Rinku Singh's Five Sixes in IPL 2023

When Kolkata Knight Riders needed 28 runs in the final over, Rinku Singh remained calm and smashed five consecutive sixes to secure an unbelievable win.

Corporate Parallel: In business, tight project deadlines demand a calm approach. Elon Musk's Tesla team faced extreme pressure to deliver the Model 3 on time, making rapid adjustments without compromising quality.

2. Handling Last-Minute Challenges

Cricket Example: Rahul Tewatia's Two Sixes in IPL 2020

With 12 runs required off the last two balls, Tewatia defied the odds, smashing two sixes to win the game for Rajasthan Royals.

Corporate Parallel: Companies dealing with last-minute client demands must act swiftly. Amazon's logistics team ensures same-day deliveries even under extreme workload, demonstrating the importance of handling pressure.

3. Staying Focused When Time is Running Out

Cricket Example: Kieron Pollard's Last-Over Heroics in T20 Matches

Pollard is known for his ability to finish games under pressure, timing his big hits perfectly to chase down targets.

Corporate Parallel: Businesses managing multiple projects must prioritize effectively. Google's AI division meets tight product development deadlines by streamlining workflow and avoiding distractions.

The Importance of Quick Execution

Management Lesson: Taking swift action at the right moment leads to a competitive advantage.

Opportunities in cricket and business are often fleeting. The ability to act decisively without over thinking separates the best from the rest.

1. Seizing the Moment

Cricket Example: Chris Gayle's 30-Ball Century in T20 Cricket

Gayle wasted no time in an IPL match, scoring the fastest T20 century, capitalizing on every ball.

Corporate Parallel: Business leaders must seize opportunities quickly. Instagram pivoted from a location-based app to a photo-sharing platform, leading to its rapid success.

2. Making Quick Adjustments

Cricket Example: Andre Russell's Power-Hitting at Any Position

Russell adapts to any match situation, whether anchoring an innings or hitting quick runs at the death.

Corporate Parallel: Startups need agility. Netflix transitioned from DVD rentals to streaming, adapting quickly to market trends.

3. Fast Decision-Making in Crisis

Cricket Example: Hardik Pandya's Bowling Change in IPL 2022

As captain, Pandya made quick tactical decisions, changing bowlers at crucial moments to ensure victory.

Corporate Parallel: CEOs must pivot strategies when necessary. During COVID-19, Zoom rapidly scaled up its services, becoming the go-to video conferencing platform.

Balancing Long-Term and Short-Term Goals

Management Lesson: A successful leader must plan for the future while managing immediate tasks.

Leaders must strike a balance between long-term vision and short-term execution to sustain growth.

1. Building a Team for the Future

Cricket Example: Mumbai Indians' Investment in Young Talent

Despite immediate setbacks, Mumbai Indians backed players like Jasprit Bumrah and Hardik Pandya, developing a team that dominated for years.

Corporate Parallel: Companies like Google invest in AI and quantum computing, ensuring future growth while maintaining current revenue streams.

2. Managing Workload for Long-Term Success

Cricket Example: Rohit Sharma's Captaincy Rotation Policy

Rohit strategically rests key players to ensure peak performance in major tournaments.

Corporate Parallel: Business leaders like Warren Buffett focus on long-term investments rather than chasing short-term profits.

3. Winning Today While Preparing for Tomorrow

Cricket Example: England's Aggressive White-Ball Cricket Transformation

England shifted from a defensive mindset to an aggressive playing style, leading to their 2019 ODI World Cup win while setting a foundation for future dominance.

Corporate Parallel: Apple continues innovating with long-term product roadmaps while keeping current products competitive in the market.

Key Takeaways for Corporate Leaders:

- **Stay Calm Under Pressure:** Focus on execution rather than fear of failure.
- **Act Quickly:** Opportunities don't wait—seize them when they arise.
- **Balance Short-Term Wins with Long-Term Vision:** Plan ahead while excelling in the present.
- **Learn from Cricket's Finishers:** Rinku Singh, Tewatia, and Pollard thrive under pressure—businesses can too.
- **Adaptability is Key:** The ability to pivot quickly ensures success in dynamic environments.

Mastering Pressure and Execution in Cricket & Business

Whether it's Rinku Singh smashing five sixes in an over, Chris Gayle executing quick fire centuries, or businesses making rapid pivots, success lies in handling pressure, executing swiftly, and balancing immediate wins with long-term goals.

By applying these principles, corporate professionals can enhance decision-making, optimize execution, and sustain long-term success—just as great cricketers manage their innings on the field.

Chapter 8

STRATEGY & PLANNING – THE ART OF EXECUTION

Management Lesson: Success depends on careful planning and flawless execution.

Strategy and planning form the backbone of success in both cricket and corporate management. The ability to assess situations, devise a clear roadmap, and execute the plan efficiently separates the best teams and businesses from the rest.

1. Long-Term Vision with Tactical Execution

Cricket Example: England's White-Ball Cricket Revolution (2015-2019)

After a disappointing 2015 World Cup exit, England adopted an aggressive white-ball strategy, building a team around players like Jos Buttler, Ben Stokes, and Jofra Archer. They planned meticulously, focusing on high strike rates, fearless cricket, and a well-balanced squad. By 2019, England executed their plan perfectly, winning their first-ever ODI World Cup.

Corporate Parallel: Successful businesses work on long-term planning. Amazon's early strategy of reinvesting profits to dominate e-commerce led to its eventual market dominance.

2. Adaptability in Execution

Cricket Example: Chennai Super Kings' IPL Success Under MS Dhoni

CSK doesn't just rely on big-name players but builds a strategy around experience, calm decision-making, and adaptability. Their ability to adjust to match situations, change batting orders, and rotate bowlers effectively has made them one of the most successful IPL teams.

Corporate Parallel: Companies like Tesla have adapted their strategies based on market conditions, shifting focus to electric vehicle production at the right time.

3. The Role of Data in Planning and Execution

Cricket Example: Mumbai Indians' Use of Data Analytics

Mumbai Indians use statistical insights to assess player performances, opposition weaknesses, and match situations. Their planning around data-driven decision-making has resulted in multiple IPL titles.

Corporate Parallel: Companies like Google and Netflix use data analytics to enhance user experience and predict customer preferences, refining their strategies based on data insights.

4. Knowing When to Take Risks and When to Play Safe

Cricket Example: Rohit Sharma's Strategic Captaincy in the 2023 Asia Cup

Rohit made calculated bowling changes and batting order decisions, knowing when to accelerate and when to consolidate, leading India to victory.

Corporate Parallel: Apple's gradual innovation strategy ensures long-term dominance, balancing risks in product design while maintaining brand reputation.

5. Execution Under Pressure – The Final Over Mentality

Cricket Example: Hardik Pandya's Leadership in IPL 2022

In his debut season as captain, Hardik led Gujarat Titans to their maiden IPL title by staying calm under pressure, making tactical field placements, and ensuring his team executed their strategies effectively in crunch moments.

Corporate Parallel: Startups and corporations need a similar approach, where CEOs make high-stakes decisions during critical phases, ensuring smooth execution under pressure.

Key Takeaways for Corporate Leaders:

- **Plan for the Long-Term:** Sustainable success requires long-term vision and planning.
- **Adapt Based on Situations:** The ability to modify strategies in real time leads to success.
- **Use Data for Decision-Making:** Insights-driven planning enhances execution.
- **Balance Risks and Stability:** Knowing when to take risks ensures steady growth.
- **Execute Under Pressure:** Success depends not just on planning but flawless execution in high-pressure situations.

Strategy and Execution – The Formula for Success

From England's white-ball transformation to Hardik Pandya's leadership, cricket proves that strategy must be backed by strong execution. In corporate settings, companies that plan efficiently, adapt when necessary, and execute with precision will achieve long-term success.

By applying these lessons, corporate professionals can improve strategic planning, enhance execution efficiency, and lead their teams toward success—just as great cricket teams do on the field.

SWOT Analysis in Cricket and Business

Management Lesson: Identifying strengths, weaknesses, opportunities, and threats is crucial for success.

A SWOT (Strengths, Weaknesses, Opportunities, and Threats) analysis helps cricket teams and businesses make informed decisions, optimize their strategies, and mitigate risks.

1. Strengths: Leveraging Key Assets

Cricket Example: Virat Kohli's Consistency as a Strength

Kohli's exceptional fitness and batting consistency across formats have been India's biggest strength, ensuring stability in key matches.

Corporate Parallel: Tata Group's strength lies in its diverse business portfolio, strong brand trust, and sustainability focus, making it a global leader.

2. Weaknesses: Identifying Areas for Improvement

Cricket Example: Pakistan's Middle-Order Fragility

Despite having world-class bowlers, Pakistan has often struggled with an inconsistent middle order, leading to collapses in crucial matches.

Corporate Parallel: Wipro identified its over-reliance on IT services and diversified into digital transformation and AI to remain competitive.

3. Opportunities: Capitalizing on Trends

Cricket Example: England's Focus on Aggressive White-Ball Cricket

Post-2015, England reinvented their limited-overs strategy, becoming a dominant force in ODIs and T20s, culminating in their 2019 World Cup win.

Corporate Parallel: Reliance Industries capitalized on India's digital revolution by launching Jio, disrupting the telecom industry and gaining massive market share.

4. Threats: Anticipating Challenges

Cricket Example: Australia's Struggle Against Spin in Subcontinent Conditions

Despite being a dominant team, Australia has historically struggled against quality spinners on Indian and Sri Lankan pitches.

Corporate Parallel: Traditional automakers like Ford and GM face threats from electric vehicle startups like Tesla, forcing them to adapt.

Planning Against Competitors

Management Lesson: Analyzing competition, identifying gaps, and developing counter-strategies lead to success.

Winning in cricket and business often depends on how well a team or company plans against its competitors.

1. Studying the Opposition's Weaknesses

Cricket Example: India's Bowling Strategy Against Steve Smith

Indian bowlers, led by Ravichandran Ashwin, executed a precise plan by targeting Smith's off-stump weakness in the 2020 Test series, leading to his early dismissals.

Corporate Parallel: Tata Motors analyzed market trends and strategically launched the Tata Nexon EV, gaining an edge in India's growing electric vehicle market.

2. Developing Custom Strategies for Different Scenarios

Cricket Example: Sri Lanka's 1996 World Cup Winning Plan

Sri Lanka introduced an aggressive opening strategy with Sanath Jayasuriya and Romesh Kaluwitharana, catching teams off guard and winning the title.

Corporate Parallel: Infosys expanded into AI-driven business solutions, ensuring they stayed ahead in IT services competition.

3. Adjusting Strategies in Real Time

Cricket Example: Rohit Sharma's Tactical Adjustments in IPL

Rohit is known for making quick fielding and bowling changes based on match situations, which has led Mumbai Indians to multiple IPL titles.

Corporate Parallel: Wipro pivoted towards AI and cloud computing when digital transformation became the industry's focal point.

Learning from Past Performances

Management Lesson: Reviewing past performances helps teams and businesses refine strategies and improve results.

The best cricket teams and companies continuously analyze their past successes and failures to refine their approach.

1. Conducting Post-Match Reviews

Cricket Example: Australia's Analysis Post-2005 Ashes Loss

After losing the 2005 Ashes, Australia revamped their training, fitness, and squad depth, regaining dominance in world cricket.

Corporate Parallel: Tata Group analyzed global trends and shifted towards sustainability and electric mobility to align with the future.

2. Learning from Failures

Cricket Example: South Africa's Choking Issue in ICC Tournaments

After multiple failures in crunch matches, South Africa introduced sports psychologists and mental training to overcome pressure situations.

Corporate Parallel: Nokia failed to adapt to smartphone trends but later learned from its mistakes, pivoting towards network and 5G technologies.

3. Adapting and Innovating Based on Past Trends

Cricket Example: India's Adaptation Post-2007 World Cup Exit

Following their early exit, India revamped their team, backed young players, and won the 2007 T20 World Cup under MS Dhoni.

Corporate Parallel: Infosys, initially a traditional IT firm, adapted by focusing on AI, blockchain, and automation to stay ahead.

Key Takeaways for Corporate Leaders:

- **SWOT Analysis Helps in Decision-Making:** Understanding strengths, weaknesses, opportunities, and threats ensures better strategy formulation.
- **Competitor Analysis is Crucial:** Studying and planning against competitors creates an edge in business and sports.
- **Review and Improve:** Learning from past performances refines future execution.
- **Adaptability Wins:** The ability to evolve after setbacks leads to long-term success.
- **Strategic Execution Matters:** Planning without execution is ineffective; action is key to success.

Learning from Cricket's Strategies for Business Success

From SWOT analysis in cricket teams to competitor planning and post-match reviews, businesses can gain valuable insights from the sport. Whether it's Tata Group's strategic expansions or Rohit Sharma's tactical IPL moves, applying these lessons ensures long-term corporate success.

By integrating these principles, corporate leaders can make informed decisions, execute strategies efficiently, and maintain a competitive edge—just as great cricket teams do on the field.

Chapter 9

RESILIENCE & COMEBACKS – BOUNCING BACK FROM SETBACKS

Management Lesson: Resilience is key to overcoming failures and achieving long-term success.

Failures and setbacks are an inevitable part of both cricket and corporate management. The ability to recover, learn from mistakes, and make a strong comeback is what defines champions.

1. Turning Setbacks into Success Stories

Cricket Example: Marvan Atapattu's Road to Success

Atapattu had a disastrous start to his Test career, scoring just one run in his first six innings. However, instead of giving up, he worked relentlessly on his technique and went on to become one of Sri Lanka's most prolific batsmen, scoring over 5,000 Test runs and leading the national team as captain.

Corporate Parallel: Steve Jobs was fired from Apple, the company he co-founded. Instead of giving up, he founded NeXT and Pixar, later returning to Apple to lead it into its most innovative era, launching the iPhone and iPad.

2. Learning from Failures and Reinventing Oneself

Cricket Example: Ben Stokes' Comeback After the 2016 T20 World Cup Final

Stokes was hit for four consecutive sixes in the final over of the 2016 T20 World Cup, leading to England's loss. Instead of letting this failure define him, he worked on his mental and physical game, making a remarkable comeback in the 2019 World Cup final, where he played a match-winning innings to secure England's first-ever World Cup title.

Corporate Parallel: Elon Musk faced multiple failures with Tesla, including production delays and financial struggles. However, through perseverance and strategic planning, Tesla became the most valuable car company in the world.

3. Overcoming Injuries and Personal Struggles

Cricket Example: Yuvraj Singh's Battle with Cancer and Triumphant Return

After being diagnosed with cancer at the peak of his career, Yuvraj Singh fought through treatment and made a comeback to international cricket, proving that resilience is not just about skill but also mental strength.

Corporate Parallel: Richard Branson, despite struggling with dyslexia, built the Virgin Group into a global brand, proving that obstacles can be turned into opportunities.

4. Reviving Careers Through Determination

Cricket Example: Dinesh Karthik's Resurgence in T20 Cricket

After years of being in and out of the Indian team, Karthik reinvented himself as a finisher in T20 cricket, earning a recall to the national side in 2022 after an impressive IPL season.

Corporate Parallel: Netflix started as a DVD rental company but transformed itself into the world's leading streaming service, adapting to new technology and market demands.

5. Leadership in Crisis and Making a Strong Return

Cricket Example: Ricky Ponting's Leadership Post-2008 Ashes Defeat

Ponting faced severe criticism after Australia lost the 2005 Ashes, but he restructured the team, worked on strategies, and led Australia to a dominant 5-0 victory in the 2006-07 Ashes series.

Corporate Parallel: Tata Motors faced a major setback with the initial failure of the Nano car but learned from the experience, focusing on innovation and launching successful models like the Tata Nexon EV.

Key Takeaways for Corporate Leaders:

- **Failures Are Stepping Stones to Success:** Embrace setbacks as learning experiences rather than barriers.
- **Work on Weaknesses to Make a Comeback:** Just as cricketers refine their techniques, businesses must innovate and adapt.
- **Stay Mentally Strong in Tough Times:** Resilience is key to overcoming challenges in both sports and business.
- **Reinvent When Necessary:** Players like Atapattu and Karthik evolved their game; companies like Netflix transformed their business models.

- **Believe in the Long-Term Vision:** Success does not come overnight—it requires patience, persistence, and adaptability.

The Power of Resilience in Cricket & Business

From Atapattu's fight for redemption to Ben Stokes' World Cup heroics, resilience defines champions. In the corporate world, leaders like Steve Jobs and Elon Musk have shown that setbacks are just stepping stones to greater success. Whether on the cricket field or in boardrooms, bouncing back stronger is what truly separates the great from the ordinary.

By applying these principles, corporate professionals can foster a resilient mindset, adapt to challenges, and drive their organizations toward sustained success—just as legendary cricketers have done on the field.

How Failures Build Stronger Professionals

Management Lesson: Failures are stepping stones to success when embraced with the right mindset.

Failure is an inevitable part of every career, be it in cricket or business. The ability to learn from setbacks and use them as fuel for growth separates successful professionals from the rest.

1. Learning from Early Career Failures

Cricket Example: Steve Smith's Evolution from Leg-Spinner to Batting Maestro

Steve Smith started his international career as a leg-spinner but struggled with inconsistency. After being dropped, he worked extensively on his batting, reinventing himself as one of the world's best batsmen, known for his unorthodox yet effective technique.

Corporate Parallel: Flipkart, an Indian e-commerce giant, started as an online bookstore but faced challenges competing with global players. Through innovation and strategy, it pivoted into a full-fledged e-commerce platform, eventually being acquired by Walmart.

2. Overcoming Setbacks to Achieve Greatness

Cricket Example: Yuvraj Singh's Journey Post-Cancer

After winning the 2011 World Cup, Yuvraj was diagnosed with cancer. He fought through treatment and made a remarkable comeback to cricket, showing that resilience and determination can overcome the toughest setbacks.

Corporate Parallel: Infosys faced near-bankruptcy in its early days but transformed itself into one of India's leading IT giants through strategic decision-making and perseverance.

Mental Toughness in Tough Situations

Management Lesson: Staying composed under pressure is what defines true leaders and performers.

The best cricketers and business leaders thrive in high-pressure situations, making clear-headed decisions when it matters most.

1. Performing Under Immense Pressure

Cricket Example: Sachin Tendulkar's 136 Against Pakistan in 1999

In a high-pressure Test match against Pakistan, Sachin played a heroic 136-run knock despite battling severe back pain. Though India fell short, his ability to focus under duress became legendary.

Corporate Parallel: Paytm CEO Vijay Shekhar Sharma faced immense challenges in competing with global payment platforms. However, his persistence and ability to handle pressure led Paytm to become India's largest digital payments company.

2. Staying Focused in a Crisis

Cricket Example: MS Dhoni's Coolness in the 2016 T20 World Cup

With 2 runs needed off the last ball against Bangladesh, Dhoni kept his cool, sprinted to the stumps, and executed a match-winning run-out, demonstrating the importance of mental composure.

Corporate Parallel: The Indian startup Zerodha revolutionized stock trading despite regulatory hurdles, proving that mental toughness and long-term vision are crucial in overcoming challenges.

Turning Criticism into Motivation

Management Lesson: Constructive criticism can be a powerful driver for success when channeled positively.

Great players and business leaders do not let criticism break them; instead, they use it as motivation to improve and prove doubters wrong.

1. Answering Critics with Performance

Cricket Example: Virat Kohli's 2014 England Tour Redemption

After a disastrous England tour in 2014 where he struggled against James Anderson, Kohli trained rigorously and returned in 2018, scoring over 500 runs in the Test series, silencing critics with his performance.

Corporate Parallel: Nykaa, India's leading beauty and wellness startup, faced skepticism initially but turned into a billion-dollar company by proving that Indian consumers were ready for a digital-first beauty marketplace.

2. Using Criticism to Fuel a Comeback

Cricket Example: Rohit Sharma's Transition to Test Opener

Rohit was often criticized for his inconsistency in Test cricket. However, after being given the role of an opener, he adapted brilliantly, scoring double centuries and becoming a crucial part of India's Test setup.

Corporate Parallel: Ola Electric faced criticism regarding its EV production timelines but used the feedback to improve and accelerate India's transition to sustainable mobility.

Key Takeaways for Corporate Leaders:

- **Failures Are Learning Opportunities:** Mistakes refine strategies and prepare professionals for greater success.
- **Mental Toughness Defines Winners:** Staying calm under pressure ensures better decision-making.

- **Use Criticism as Fuel:** Let negativity push you toward excellence rather than discouragement.
- **Adaptability is Key to Growth:** Whether it's Steve Smith switching from a bowler to a world-class batsman or a startup pivoting its business model, adaptability ensures success.
- **Composure in Tough Moments Brings Clarity:** Just like Dhoni's last-ball run-out or Sachin's match-saving knocks, business leaders must remain calm to navigate challenges effectively.

Building Strength Through Challenges

From Sachin Tendulkar's resilience to Steve Smith's career reinvention, cricket teaches us that setbacks are not failures—they are stepping stones to success. Similarly, companies like Flipkart, Nykaa, and Ola Electric have turned obstacles into opportunities through perseverance and smart decision-making.

By applying these principles, corporate professionals can cultivate resilience, improve mental toughness, and use criticism as a stepping stone to success—just as legendary cricketers have done on the field.

Chapter 10

ETHICS & FAIR PLAY IN BUSINESS

Management Lesson: Integrity, fairness, and ethical leadership build long-term trust and success.

In both cricket and business, ethics and fair play are essential for maintaining trust and sustainability. Success achieved through honesty, respect, and adherence to rules is far more valuable than short-term gains through unethical practices.

1. Leading with Integrity

Cricket Example: Kane Williamson's Sportsmanship in the 2019 World Cup

Kane Williamson and the New Zealand cricket team demonstrated exceptional integrity during the 2019 World Cup final against England. Despite losing the match in controversial circumstances due to an unusual boundary count rule, Williamson accepted the result with grace, setting an example of sportsmanship and fairness.

Corporate Parallel: The Tata Group has built its reputation on ethical leadership and integrity. From Ratan Tata's decision to maintain employee salaries during the 2008 recession to the group's commitment to social responsibility, Tata has always prioritized ethics over short-term profits.

2. Respecting Rules and Playing Fair

Cricket Example: New Zealand's Fair Play Culture

New Zealand cricket is known for playing the game in the right spirit. Unlike teams that engage in sledging or questionable tactics, the Kiwis focus on competing with respect and fairness, earning global admiration.

Corporate Parallel: Infosys, one of India's leading IT firms, has maintained transparency and ethical business practices despite market pressures. Its founder, Narayana Murthy, established a culture of honesty and fairness, ensuring Infosys became synonymous with corporate ethics.

3. Handling Controversies with Honesty

Cricket Example: Adam Gilchrist's 'Walking' Decision

In the 2003 World Cup semifinal, Australian wicketkeeper-batsman Adam Gilchrist walked off the field despite the umpire not giving him out. His decision to uphold the spirit of the game over personal or team gains earned him immense respect.

Corporate Parallel: The Mahindra Group, led by Anand Mahindra, has always taken a transparent approach to business. The company openly acknowledges mistakes and rectifies them rather than hiding ethical lapses, reinforcing customer trust.

4. Ethical Decision-Making in High-Stakes Moments

Cricket Example: Rahul Dravid's Approach to Coaching

As India's U19 and National Cricket Academy coach, Dravid emphasizes character-building alongside skill development. He ensures that young cricketers learn the values of respect, honesty, and discipline, helping shape responsible athletes.

Corporate Parallel: Wipro, under Azim Premji's leadership, has built a legacy of corporate responsibility. The company has been committed to philanthropy and ethical governance, ensuring business growth aligns with societal well-being.

5. The Cost of Ethical Failures

Cricket Example: The 2018 Australian Ball-Tampering Scandal

Steve Smith, David Warner, and Cameron Bancroft were involved in a ball-tampering scandal, leading to widespread condemnation and suspensions. This incident damaged Australia's cricketing reputation, proving that unethical actions have long-term consequences.

Corporate Parallel: The Satyam Computers scandal, where financial fraud led to the collapse of the company, is a reminder that unethical business practices can destroy trust and credibility. However, the company's revival under the Mahindra Group highlighted the importance of restoring ethics in business.

Key Takeaways for Corporate Leaders:

- **Integrity Builds Trust:** Ethical leadership fosters long-term success and respect.
- **Fair Play Strengthens Brand Reputation:** Playing by the rules enhances a company's credibility.
- **Handling Setbacks with Grace is Key:** Accepting failures ethically, like New Zealand did in 2019, sets an example for others.
- **Honesty is the Best Policy:** Organizations that maintain transparency, like Tata and Wipro, thrive in the long run.
- **Unethical Actions Have Consequences:** Scandals in both sports and business damage credibility and take years to rebuild.

The Role of Ethics in Long-Term Success

Whether in cricket or corporate management, integrity and fair play define true winners. Leaders like Kane Williamson and companies like Tata and Infosys have proven that ethical leadership leads to long-term success.

By applying these principles, corporate professionals can create an environment of trust, foster a positive brand image, and ensure sustained growth—just as ethical cricketing teams do on the field.

How Ethical Leadership Builds Trust

Management Lesson: Ethical leadership fosters loyalty, credibility, and long-term success.

In both cricket and corporate management, trust is the foundation of sustainable success. Leaders who prioritize integrity and fair play earn respect and build lasting relationships.

1. Leading by Example

Cricket Example: Kane Williamson's Grace in the 2019 World Cup Final

Despite losing in controversial circumstances, Williamson displayed exceptional humility, accepting the result without protest. His conduct earned admiration worldwide, proving that true leadership is about grace under pressure.

Corporate Parallel: The Tata Group, under Ratan Tata, has always prioritized ethical business practices. Even when facing competition, the company maintained fair practices, gaining immense trust among stakeholders and customers.

2. Transparency and Honesty in Decision-Making

Cricket Example: Rahul Dravid's Approach to Team Management

Dravid, as a player and coach, has always emphasized integrity, mentoring young cricketers to uphold sportsmanship and ethical conduct both on and off the field.

Corporate Parallel: Infosys, under Narayana Murthy, built its reputation on transparent governance and ethical decision-making, ensuring long-term stability and trust.

Corporate Scandals vs. Fair Play in Business

Management Lesson: Ethical failures lead to long-term consequences, while fair play builds lasting credibility.

Success achieved through unethical means often results in reputational damage, as seen in both cricketing scandals and corporate frauds.

1. The Cost of Cheating in Cricket

Cricket Example: Australian Sandpaper Gate Scandal (2018)

Australian cricketers Steve Smith, David Warner, and Cameron Bancroft were caught using sandpaper to tamper with the ball during a Test match against South Africa. The scandal led to suspensions, loss of sponsorships, and widespread condemnation.

Corporate Parallel: The Volkswagen emissions scandal, where the company manipulated emissions data, resulted in billions of dollars in fines and a significant loss of public trust.

2. The Damage of Repeated Ethical Violations

Cricket Example: Shahid Afridi's Ball-Tampering Incident

In 2010, Afridi was caught biting the ball to alter its condition. His actions resulted in a ban and criticism, damaging his credibility as a leader.

Corporate Parallel: The Satyam Computers scandal saw the company's CEO manipulate financial records, leading to a corporate collapse. However, under new ethical leadership (Mahindra Group), the company was revived as Tech Mahindra.

3. Fair Play and Corporate Success

Cricket Example: New Zealand's Ethical Approach to Cricket

New Zealand's cricket team consistently upholds fair play principles, earning the ICC Spirit of Cricket award multiple times.

Corporate Parallel: Wipro, known for its ethical governance and CSR initiatives, has sustained a positive corporate image, reinforcing the value of ethical leadership.

The Importance of Honesty and Sportsmanship

Management Lesson: Ethical conduct fosters loyalty, respect, and long-term growth.

Cricket and business leaders who value honesty and fair play inspire confidence and loyalty among their teams, customers, and fans.

1. Honesty Strengthens Reputation

Cricket Example: Adam Gilchrist's Decision to Walk in the 2003 World Cup

Despite the umpire not giving him out, Gilchrist walked off the field voluntarily, reinforcing the importance of honesty in cricket.

Corporate Parallel: Mahindra Group, led by Anand Mahindra, has built a reputation for integrity, ensuring ethical practices in all business dealings.

2. Handling Setbacks with Integrity

Cricket Example: Anil Kumble's Response to the 2008 Sydney Test Controversy

Despite questionable umpiring decisions against India, Kumble maintained composure, famously stating, "Only one team was playing in the spirit of the game."

Corporate Parallel: Infosys, after facing leadership challenges, ensured a smooth transition while maintaining its core ethical principles.

3. Ethical Conduct Brings Long-Term Success

Cricket Example: MS Dhoni's Captaincy Style

Dhoni's leadership was built on fairness, trust, and respect. His commitment to fair play made him one of the most respected leaders in cricket.

Corporate Parallel: HDFC Bank has consistently adhered to ethical banking practices, earning customer trust and industry leadership.

Key Takeaways for Corporate Leaders:

- **Ethical Leadership Builds Trust:** Leaders like Kane Williamson and Ratan Tata demonstrate that integrity fosters long-term success.
- **Cheating Leads to Consequences:** The Australian sandpaper scandal and Volkswagen emissions fraud highlight the dangers of unethical practices.
- **Fair Play Enhances Brand Value:** Companies like Infosys and Wipro thrive by maintaining ethical standards.
- **Honesty and Sportsmanship Matter:** Just as Gilchrist walked when given not out, businesses that uphold transparency earn customer loyalty.
- **Integrity Ensures Longevity:** Ethical governance, as seen in Tata and Mahindra, results in sustained business success.

Ethics as the Cornerstone of Success

From Williamson's sportsmanship to Dhoni's fair play, cricket teaches us that ethical leadership fosters respect and credibility. In the corporate world, Tata, Infosys, and Wipro exemplify how integrity leads to long-term prosperity.

By integrating these principles, corporate professionals can cultivate trust, maintain transparency, and drive sustainable success—just as great cricketers have done on the field.

Chapter 11

CONCLUSION: FROM GULLY CRICKET TO CORPORATE BOARDROOMS

Management Lesson: Success is a journey of resilience, strategic execution, and teamwork.

Cricket is not just a sport – it is a microcosm of life and business. The journey from **gully cricket to the corporate boardroom** embodies the spirit of growth, adaptability, and leadership. The lessons learned in the narrow lanes of childhood matches – quick thinking, teamwork, risk management, and strategic execution – become essential skills in the business world.

Many of today's cricket stars started from humble beginnings, just like entrepreneurs who built successful companies from small ideas. The struggles, triumphs, and learnings along the way shape them into world-class performers, just as corporate leaders evolve through experience and resilience.

1. From Humble Beginnings to Global Success

Cricket Example: Tilak Varma's Journey from Tennis Ball Cricket to the IPL

Tilak Varma, a young cricketer from Hyderabad, started playing in the narrow streets and small grounds before being discovered. His hard work and perseverance led him to become one of the most promising young batters in the IPL.

Corporate Parallel: Boat, co-founded by **Aman Gupta,** began as a small consumer electronics brand and is now one of India's biggest lifestyle electronics companies, showing that persistence and vision can take a company from an idea to an industry leader.

2. Adaptability: Thriving in Changing Environments

Cricket Example: Ruturaj Gaikwad's Adaptation to Different Formats

Gaikwad went from being a classical red-ball cricketer to excelling as an opener in T20 cricket. His ability to adjust to different formats and conditions showcases how flexibility is key to success.

Corporate Parallel: Zomato started as a restaurant discovery platform but quickly pivoted into **food delivery and cloud kitchens** to keep up with market demands, proving that businesses must evolve to stay relevant.

3. Handling Pressure and Bouncing Back

Cricket Example: Yashasvi Jaiswal's Rise After Early Struggles

Jaiswal, once living in tents and selling street food to fund his cricket career, turned his life around through sheer dedication. His breakout IPL and domestic performances made him a rising star for India.

Corporate Parallel: Udaan, a B2B e-commerce startup, struggled with financial setbacks but **reinvented its operations,** ensuring steady growth in India's business marketplace.

4. Building a Strong Team for Long-Term Success

Cricket Example: India's 2023 ODI World Cup Strategy

India built a **balanced, well-structured team** with experienced players and young talent. The team's cohesion and role clarity contributed to its dominant run in the tournament.

Corporate Parallel: Razorpay, one of India's leading fintech startups, assembled a strong team focused on financial innovation, driving exponential growth in the online payments industry.

5. Leadership, Ethics, and Long-Term Vision

Cricket Example: Shreyas Iyer's Composed Captaincy in the IPL

Iyer showcased leadership at a young age, guiding his team with calmness and tactical brilliance, proving that vision and discipline matter in building a successful unit.

Corporate Parallel: CRED, founded by **Kunal Shah,** disrupted India's credit market by focusing on rewarding financial discipline, proving that ethical business practices can lead to long-term brand loyalty and success.

Key Takeaways for Future Leaders:

- **Start Small, Dream Big:** Like Tilak Varma and Boat, every success story begins with an idea and hard work.
- **Adapt to Change:** Success depends on flexibility, as seen in Gaikwad's career shift and Zomato's business transformation.
- **Turn Struggles into Strengths:** Jaiswal and Udaan proved that resilience creates new opportunities.

- **Teamwork Drives Performance:** India's cricket strategy and Razorpay's fintech success highlight the importance of strong teams.
- **Lead with Ethics and Innovation:** Just as Iyer and CRED's Kunal Shah demonstrated, sustainable success is built on vision, ethics, and innovation.

Final Thoughts: Bridging Cricket and Corporate Leadership

The journey from **gully cricket to corporate boardrooms** is not just about talent—it's about persistence, adaptability, teamwork, and ethical leadership. The same qualities that make a player a great cricketer also make a professional a great leader.

Whether you are an aspiring cricketer or an entrepreneur, the path is the same—**stay committed, take smart risks, learn from failures, and build a strong team.** The next world-class cricketer could be playing in the streets today, just as the next business leader could be working on an innovative idea in a small workspace.

So, **play every game with passion, work with integrity, and never stop learning—because every challenge is just a stepping stone to success.**

How Childhood Cricket Experiences Shape Management Thinking

Management Lesson: The early lessons learned on the cricket field influence problem-solving, decision-making, and leadership skills in business.

Many corporate leaders grew up playing cricket, unknowingly developing skills that later helped them excel in business. The quick decision-making in a last-over chase, the ability to handle pressure when batting with one wicket left, or the need for clear communication between running batsmen—all these experiences shape a leader's mindset and management approach.

1. Decision-Making Under Pressure

Cricket Example: Rishabh Pant's fearless approach in Test cricket

Pant's ability to make bold decisions, like stepping out to fast bowlers in crucial moments, showcases how early confidence and risk-taking develop leadership skills.

Corporate Parallel: Business leaders, much like cricketers, must make quick decisions under uncertainty. **Byju's,** which started as a small coaching business, took a risk by digitizing education and became India's largest EdTech company.

2. Resourcefulness and Adaptability

Cricket Example: Shubman Gill's adaptation across formats

Gill has successfully transitioned between Test, ODI, and T20 cricket, showing adaptability—a key trait in business leadership.

Corporate Parallel: Companies like **Zepto,** which pioneered **10-minute grocery delivery,** show how rapid adaptation to market needs leads to business success.

3. Managing Teams and Building Trust

Cricket Example: Hardik Pandya's leadership at Gujarat Titans

Pandya was an unexpected IPL captain but thrived by trusting his teammates and executing plans efficiently.

Corporate Parallel: Freshworks, an Indian SaaS company, succeeded globally by empowering employees and creating a strong culture of collaboration.

The Importance of Continuous Learning and Adapting

Management Lesson: Just as cricket evolves, so does business—learning and adaptability are crucial for long-term success.

Cricket is a game of constant evolution. Formats have changed from five-day Test matches to ODIs and fast-paced T20 leagues. Similarly, businesses must innovate and adapt to remain competitive.

1. Learning from Failures and Bouncing Back

Cricket Example: Virat Kohli's redemption after the 2014 England tour

After a disastrous series against England, Kohli worked on his technique and returned stronger, dominating world cricket.

Corporate Parallel: Paytm faced regulatory challenges but adapted by diversifying its offerings into UPI transactions and digital banking.

2. Reinventing Strategies

Cricket Example: England's white-ball revolution post-2015

After a humiliating early exit in the 2015 World Cup, England changed their approach, embracing aggressive batting, leading to their 2019 World Cup victory.

Corporate Parallel: OYO Rooms initially struggled with its business model but adjusted its expansion strategy, focusing on sustainable growth and profitability.

3. Investing in Skill Development

Cricket Example: India's U-19 talent development under Rahul Dravid

Dravid's focus on nurturing young players ensured that India's pipeline of cricketing talent remained strong.

Corporate Parallel: Tata Group continuously invests in research and development, ensuring it stays ahead in industries like automobiles (Tata Motors EVs) and technology (TCS AI solutions).

Final Thoughts on Why Every Manager Should Play or Follow Cricket

Management Lesson: Cricket provides valuable insights into leadership, resilience, and teamwork—qualities essential for corporate success.

Cricket is more than a sport; it is a **strategic battlefield, a team-building exercise, and a masterclass in leadership.** Every manager, whether leading a small team or a multinational corporation, can learn invaluable management lessons by either playing or following the game.

1. Understanding Team Dynamics

Cricket teaches that individual brilliance alone doesn't win games—teams do. Managers who understand this foster collaboration in workplaces.

2. Strategic Thinking in High-Pressure Situations

Watching how a captain plans field placements or manages bowling rotations can teach managers about tactical decision-making in business.

3. Learning to Handle Unpredictability

Every match is different, just like every business challenge is unique. Cricket teaches adaptability, helping managers stay calm under uncertainty.

4. Building a Winning Culture

Successful cricket teams focus on **process over results.** Companies that prioritize innovation and long-term goals build **winning corporate cultures** that sustain growth.

Final Words for Managers and Employees

Whether you play cricket in your free time, watch it passionately, or simply follow the strategies of great captains, the game has **endless lessons** to offer for personal and professional growth. Just as cricketers sharpen their skills every day, managers and employees must continuously learn, adapt, and **play to win.**

So, the next time you watch a match, don't just admire the sixes and wickets—observe the leadership, strategy, and teamwork at play. Because whether in cricket or business, the **real champions are those who think ahead, take bold steps, and work together to achieve greatness.**

Management Lesson: Success is a journey of resilience, strategic execution, and teamwork.

Cricket is not just a sport—it is a microcosm of life and business. The journey from **gully cricket to the corporate boardroom** embodies the spirit of growth, adaptability, and leadership. The lessons learned in the narrow lanes of childhood matches—quick thinking, teamwork, risk management, and strategic execution—become essential skills in the business world.

Many of today's cricket stars started from humble beginnings, just like entrepreneurs who built successful companies from small ideas. The struggles, triumphs, and learnings along the way shape them into world-class performers, just as corporate leaders evolve through experience and resilience.

1. From Humble Beginnings to Global Success

Cricket Example: Tilak Varma's Journey from Tennis Ball Cricket to the IPL

Tilak Varma, a young cricketer from Hyderabad, started playing in the narrow streets and small grounds before being discovered. His hard work and perseverance led him to become one of the most promising young batters in the IPL.

Corporate Parallel: Boat, co-founded by **Aman Gupta,** began as a small consumer electronics brand and is now one of India's biggest lifestyle electronics companies, showing that persistence and vision can take a company from an idea to an industry leader.

2. Adaptability: Thriving in Changing Environments

Cricket Example: Ruturaj Gaikwad's Adaptation to Different Formats

Gaikwad went from being a classical red-ball cricketer to excelling as an opener in T20 cricket. His ability to adjust to different formats and conditions showcases how flexibility is key to success.

Corporate Parallel: Zomato started as a restaurant discovery platform but quickly pivoted into **food delivery and cloud kitchens** to keep up with market demands, proving that businesses must evolve to stay relevant.

3. Handling Pressure and Bouncing Back

Cricket Example: Yashasvi Jaiswal's Rise After Early Struggles

Jaiswal, once living in tents and selling street food to fund his cricket career, turned his life around through sheer dedication. His breakout IPL and domestic performances made him a rising star for India.

Corporate Parallel: Udaan, a B2B e-commerce startup, struggled with financial setbacks but **reinvented its operations,** ensuring steady growth in India's business marketplace.

4. Building a Strong Team for Long-Term Success

Cricket Example: India's 2023 ODI World Cup Strategy

India built a **balanced, well-structured team** with experienced players and young talent. The team's cohesion and role clarity contributed to its dominant run in the tournament.

Corporate Parallel: Razorpay, one of India's leading fintech startups, assembled a strong team focused on financial innovation, driving exponential growth in the online payments industry.

5. Leadership, Ethics, and Long-Term Vision

Cricket Example: Shreyas Iyer's Composed Captaincy in the IPL

Iyer showcased leadership at a young age, guiding his team with calmness and tactical brilliance, proving that vision and discipline matter in building a successful unit.

Corporate Parallel: CRED, founded by **Kunal Shah,** disrupted India's credit market by focusing on rewarding financial discipline, proving that ethical business practices can lead to long-term brand loyalty and success.

Key Takeaways for Future Leaders:

- **Start Small, Dream Big:** Like Tilak Varma and Boat, every success story begins with an idea and hard work.
- **Adapt to Change:** Success depends on flexibility, as seen in Gaikwad's career shift and Zomato's business transformation.
- **Turn Struggles into Strengths:** Jaiswal and Udaan proved that resilience creates new opportunities.
- **Teamwork Drives Performance:** India's cricket strategy and Razorpay's fintech success highlight the importance of strong teams.
- **Lead with Ethics and Innovation:** Just as Iyer and CRED's Kunal Shah demonstrated, sustainable success is built on vision, ethics, and innovation.